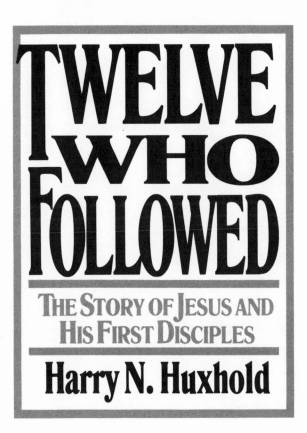

TWELVE WHO FOLLOWED

THE STORY OF JESUS AND HIS FIRST DISCIPLES

Harry N. Huxhold

AUGSBURG Publishing House • Minneapolis

To
James Bartholomew

TWELVE WHO FOLLOWED
The Story of Jesus and His First Disciples

Copyright © 1987 Augsburg Publishing House

Scripture quotations unless otherwise noted are from the Holy Bible: New International Version. Copyright 1978 by the New York International Bible Society. Used by permission of Zondervan Bible Publishers.

Library of Congress Cataloging-in-Publication Data

Huxhold, Harry N.
 TWELVE WHO FOLLOWED.

 1. Apostles—Bibliography.   I. Title.
BS2440.H88   1987   226'.0922 [B]   86-30218
ISBN 0-8066-2242-3

Manufactured in the U.S.A.   APH 10-6722

     3   4   5   6   7   8   9   0   1   2   3   4   5   6   7   8   9

CONTENTS

My command is this: Love each other as I have loved you. Greater love has no one than this, that one lay down his life for his friends. You are my friends if you do what I command. I no longer call you servants, because a servant does not know his master's business. Instead, I have called you friends, for everything that I learned from my Father I have made known to you. You did not choose me, but I chose you to go and bear fruit—fruit that will last. Then the Father will give you whatever you ask in my name. This is my command: Love each other.

John 15:12-17

ONE

WHY THE TWELVE?

When Edgar J. Goodspeed, New Testament scholar and translator of both the Old and the New Testaments, was invited to write a book about the 12 apostles, he hesitated. He realized that our information about the apostles is so scanty that one would be hard-pressed to fill out even an obituary notice for most of them. But on second thought, he decided that the apostles had been effective in carrying out the commission the Lord had given them to evangelize the world, and the materials we do have give us some insights into their lives and activities.

The fact that we do not have a record of everything that happened does not mean nothing took place. We don't always know who went where and who did what, but we know that the Word got out. That was not by accident, but followed God's plan in choosing the Twelve. To them he entrusted this task of sharing the revelation which God made in the life, death, and resurrection of Jesus of Nazareth.

Twelve Is Symbolic

That Jesus chose 12 apostles is not surprising. The number 12 figures prominently in the Scriptures. There are 12 years, 12 wells in Elim, 12 silver bowls, 12 golden spoons, 12 bullocks, and many other uses of the number. In addition, there are the multiples of 12.

There were also 12 tribes of Israel, and when Jesus chose 12 apostles, he wanted everyone to understand that he was guaranteeing the continuation of God's mercy through a new Israel. As the patriarchs had been promised that in Israel all nations of the earth would be blessed, so the promise would come to its fulfillment in a new Israel that would be a blessing to many. The apostles were to assist our Lord in his mission of building the kingdom and in the future judgment (Matt. 19:28). When Judas Iscariot was lost to the group, the vacancy was filled with the inclusion of Matthias. The group was then closed; no other names were ever to be added to the Twelve.

Twelve for Witness

While the number of the disciples had significance for the new Israel, there were precedents for the creation of a band of disciples. The prophet Isaiah had realized the practical value of gathering disciples around himself. Isaiah proclaimed, "Bind up the testimony and seal up the law among my disciples" (Isa. 8:16). The prophet's disciples were the ones who gathered, preserved, and protected the sermons, oracles, poems, and hymns of the prophet. They were the witnesses to his ministry and heard his preaching and teaching. Their devotion to their leader prompted them to memorialize the work of their teacher so that it would not be lost. This was that model that Jesus emulated when he chose the 12 disciples.

Jesus not only exercised his prerogative to choose his disciples, but he also painstakingly instructed them with the same goal Isaiah had for his disciples. The Twelve were not only to benefit from his teaching and ministry, but they were to be an integral part of that ministry. They were the people in whom Jesus could invest himself and his love. They were the ones to whom he could entrust his teaching. They were the ones who could testify what God had done in sending this special Son.

Witnesses

Having said all that, we are struck with the paucity of material we have from the Twelve. Few of the Twelve actually wrote, and what we do have is not history as we know it. Nor is it biography or autobiography as we think of those forms today. What we have is witness. What the Twelve gave us was their witness to the grace and mercy of God as it was manifested in the life, death, and resurrection of Jesus. What we have is not extraneous to the history of our salvation. It focuses on the heart of the matter, God's heart as it was exposed to the world in Jesus. This witness was given for us not only in what was recorded, but also in the lively oral witness the Twelve gave to the gospel before anything was written.

The fact that there was an immediate continuation of the Lord's ministry in the lives of the Twelve was a witness in itself. They did not fail in the purpose for which Jesus called them when he followed Isaiah in sealing his teaching among his disciples.

The Twelve obeyed Jesus' instruction that they begin the preaching of his gospel in Jerusalem and Judea. However, because of the persecution that began in Jerusalem, they soon found themselves preaching the gospel in territories that were strange to them. Paul, who began his public career as a chief persecutor of the Christians, found it necessary to pursue the Christians as far away as Damascus. Later, when Paul himself became an apostle, he wrote to a congregation of Christians at Rome. The gospel had already traveled across the seas to the capital of the empire.

The first generation of Christians was driven by a conviction that the Lord would return in glory within their lifetime. They did not take time to write about their experiences or record the history of their movement; they were busy preaching repentance of sin and faith in the crucified and risen Lord.

The first writings of the Christians were letters to specific congregations and letters to be circulated among all the Christians in dealing with the practical problems and questions that this new way of living and believing raised among them. With the passing of the first generation it became apparent that those who were able should record the Christ event. Of the four Gospels, tradition assigns Matthew to the disciple named Matthew, the Gospel of Mark to a disciple of Peter, Luke to a disciple of Paul, and John to a disciple of the apostle John.

The writers of the New Testament gathered the materials that were the *kerygma*, the proclamation of God's love in Jesus Christ. They were not interested in simply giving data or facts. They told what was necessary to remind us of the depths and profundity of our sin. Our unfaith, our unbelief, our rebellion against God, and our self-centeredness are so ingrained and pervasive that we are slaves to sin. Our only hope of rescue from death and hell is in the mercy and grace of God. That grace is revealed most clearly in Jesus. Nowhere else can we both learn so much about God and ourselves and have such reason to trust God's goodness.

It was only natural that the church was curious as to how the Twelve spread this good news as well and as quickly as they did. Some began to fill in the gaps in what was known with some pious tales that may or may not be authentic. Spurious gospels and books of acts of the apostles began to appear. As we read those materials we can easily sort out the fanciful and romantic because so much of that material contradicts the New Testament.

Why They Were Chosen

We can understand why the disciples left us the materials they did and why they did not leave accounts of their own accomplishments. Already in their calling by Jesus it was clear that their presence with the Lord was not dependent on their initiative. In rabbinical circles it was customary for the disciples to choose their teacher, but Jesus chose his disciples. His act of grace in choosing them elicited their response of faith. They were under no compulsion, but his persuasive manner created a relationship that was sealed by his continuing love for them.

What recommended the Twelve for discipleship was the fact that they had nothing to offer. Over and over they showed how empty-headed they could be. But they did not have empty hearts. Jesus had filled them with his love, which assured them that he was truly of God and that the call he had issued to them was from God. The disciples were caught up in a faith relationship that made them a part of God's kingdom. As different as they all were, they had this faith in common. They could feel tensions between themselves, but not with Jesus. They belonged to him because he had first loved them (John 15:16).

Why We Are Chosen

We become believers in the same way. We come empty-handed, with nothing to offer God to persuade him to make us his own. We love God because he first loved us in Christ, who died for us while we were yet sinners. We belong to that succession of believers who follow the disciples who walked in the footsteps of our Lord. With the calling of these 12 people Jesus established the New Israel. Just as an entire nation of people had been the descendants of the 12 sons of Jacob, now a new and holy nation are the spiritual descendants of the 12 apostles. As the messianic hope and promise had been carried forward in a people, now the fulfillment of that promise continues in us.

In that sense we are a part of a mission that is dependent on us. As Jesus relied on these homely, ordinary, first-century men to carry on his work, which he entrusted to them with the confidence that God's Spirit would make something of the message they shared, God does the same with us. He makes disciples of us, shoves us out into the world, hoping for the best from us, because he has given us his Spirit. We may not do any better than the disciples, or look any more brilliant, or give off any more flashes of excitement, but Christ will work through us.

When Jesus came to the district of Caesarea Philippi, he asked his disciples, "Who do people say the Son of Man is?"

They replied, "Some say John the Baptist; others say Elijah; and still others, Jeremiah or one of the prophets."

"But what about you?" he asked.

Simon Peter answered, "You are the Christ, the Son of the living God."

Jesus replied, "Blessed are you, Simon son of Jonah, for this was not revealed to you by man, but by my Father in heaven. And I tell you that you are Peter, and on this rock I will build my church, and the gates of Hades will not overcome it. I will give you the keys of the kingdom of heaven; whatever you bind on earth will be bound in heaven, and whatever you loose on earth will be loosed in heaven."

Matthew 16:13-19

TWO

PETER, NUMBER ONE

They called him "the Big Fisherman," and so he was. We do not know how tall Peter was, but he stood tall among all his colleagues. We do not know how much he weighed, but he knew how to throw his weight around. Whenever we try to picture him, we have to draw Peter in heroic proportions. He was a naturally born leader.

Peter was rarely at a loss for words. He took risks. He blundered, but after making a buffoon of himself, he recovered. He was filled with compassion and warmth. He could make you feel embarrassed for him, but he could just as easily win your admiration.

We stand in awe of people like Peter, because they are not afraid of life. We are inclined to follow such people because they are persons of action who know how to build our confidence and inspire us to act. We know that such leaders may have feet of clay, and there are things about them we may not like, but there they are, right up front, and we do not know anyone who can do better.

Front and Center

That is exactly how the disciples thought of Peter. Every catalog of the disciples lists Peter first. He was number one, as the spokesman for the Twelve. He is also first in terms of the number of biblical references. We know more about Peter than of any of the others. We have more speeches from him than all the others.

Many events in the life of Jesus seem to center around Peter. We get the impression that Peter offered his home as a headquarters for Jesus while he was in the area of Capernaum (Mark 1:29). It was Peter's boat that was pressed into service whenever the Lord was at the seashore.

The other disciples, willingly or grudgingly, allowed Peter to exercise leadership among them. What is more notable is the fact that Jesus himself gave Peter his place among the disciples. After Jesus ascended, Peter continued to serve as a leader of the early church.

That Peter attained such prominence among the Twelve and later as a chief apostle of the church is remarkable. He was an unlikely candidate for discipleship. He came from Bethsaida, which is Hebrew for the "House of Nets"—a fisherman's town. Our Lord's detractors did not hesitate to make a great deal of the fact that disciples like Peter were uneducated people. After Jesus' ascension these enemies continued to make note of that (Acts 4:13). However, it should be noted that Peter came from an area in which the people knew and spoke Greek. The territory was Hebrew, but the people were influenced by Greek culture.

Peter's real name in Hebrew would have been Symeon. However, most often he is called Simon, a Greek name. His brother Andrew and another disciple, Philip, also had Greek names. *Peter* is the name our Lord conferred on Simon (Mark 3:16). Peter is really a descriptive title. In

Aramaic the word is *Kepha* and means "stone" or "rock." Using Greek letters to transliterate the word, it comes out *Cephas*. Translated into Greek, the word is *Petros*. He is also known as Simon Bar-Jona—that is, Simon, son of John.

His Confession

A few events help us understand Peter's place among the disciples.

Once Peter told Jesus that they had toiled all night and had caught no fish. Then he added, "But because you say so, I will let down the nets" (Luke 5:5). When Peter and the others hauled in a great catch of fish, Peter fell down at Jesus' knees and said, "Go away from me, Lord; I am a sinful man!"

Jesus then called Peter to be an apostle. "Don't be afraid; from now on you will catch men."

Later, when many defected from following Jesus, he asked the Twelve, "Will you also go away?"

Peter spoke up for the group: "Lord, to whom shall we go? You have the words of eternal life. We believe and know that you are the Holy One of God" (John 6:68-69). Illiterate or not, Peter discerned Jesus' messianic role. Peter and the other disciples could look like chumps and be stupid about many things, but they recognized that their association with Jesus was out of the ordinary. They felt and knew the presence of God in this man of Nazareth. This understanding was an extraordinary gift of God (Matt. 16:17).

Leader of the Early Church

After Christ's ascension, Peter continued his leadership role. Paul reported that the risen Lord appeared first to

Cephas and then to the Twelve (1 Cor. 15:5). Peter recovered from his denial of Jesus through repentance and receiving absolution from the risen Christ (John 21). After the Lord's ascension, Peter took charge of the eleven remaining disciples and urged them to elect a 12th to take the place of Judas Iscariot. From that time on Peter appears to have presided over the small group.

At Pentecost Peter once more rose to the occasion. In a brilliant sermon on the meaning of the life, death, and resurrection of Jesus he created a model for apostolic preaching.

Peter continued to lead the early church at Jerusalem through a succession of events that included his own imprisonment and release through miraculous intervention (Acts 5:19). Peter was the chief defender of the faith in the face of the opposition and authorities. He also exercised church discipline in the cases of Ananias and Sapphira (Acts 5:1-11) and Simon (Acts 8:14-24). Peter was also singled out as the one representative of the Lord's healing ministry as it continued in the life of the early church (Acts 5:12-16).

Peter the Missionary

Under Peter's leadership the Christian movement was so widespread that people began to suffer persecution for their confession of faith in Christ. After the stoning of Stephen, Christians were scattered and carried the gospel wherever they went. Though the Twelve appeared to enjoy some form of sanctuary in Jerusalem, Peter was soon called on to assist in other areas. He appeared first at Lydda and Joppa (Acts 9:32-43).

Peter is also credited with being the first to serve as a missionary to a Gentile, the centurion Cornelius (Acts 10).

Later Peter was imprisoned once more and again miraculously liberated. On his release he left for "another place" (Acts 12:17).

From that point on, Peter was replaced as the administrative head in Jerusalem by James, the brother of our Lord (Acts 15:12-21). Peter was still regarded as one of the pillars of the church, but he was now in charge of the mission to the Jews (Gal. 2:7-9). His wife evidently traveled with him on his journeys (1 Cor. 9:5). It has been suggested that he helped to establish the church at Antioch. The fact that Paul mentions that there was a Cephas party in Corinth suggests that he may also have gone there.

Martyred for the Faith

We do not know for sure where else Peter's missionary journeys may have taken him. However, tradition places his last days in Rome. Oscar Cullmann, a Swiss scholar of the New Testament, made a careful examination of biblical, traditional, and archeological data and concluded that Peter probably died a martyr in Rome under a persecution by Nero about A.D. 65. According to tradition, since Peter lacked the credentials and safeguards of Roman citizenship that Paul had, he was crucified (upside down, by his own request). We have good reason to believe that before his martyr's death Peter was the narrator of the events recorded in the gospel of Mark. The gospel reveals the heavy imprint of Peter's influence from beginning to end.

A Rock for the Church

In response to Jesus' query, "Who do you say that I am?" Peter confessed the faith of the church: "You are the Christ, the Son of the Living God" (Matt. 16:16).

Jesus replied, "Blessed are you, Simon son of Jonah, for this was not revealed to you by man, but by my Father in heaven. And I tell you that you are Peter, and on this rock I will build my church, and the gates of Hades will not overcome it. I will give you the keys of the kingdom of heaven; whatever you bind on earth will be bound in heaven, and whatever you loose on earth will be loosed in heaven."

Peter did become a rock for the church. Not only did he give solid leadership to the early church, but he became a rock in the manner in which he defended the faith and became an apostle of hope for the church in time of distress and persecution. The epistles of Peter indicate the kind of hope he held out to the church. On the foundation of the apostolic faith exemplified by Peter, Christ continues to build his church. Our link with Peter is this same faith that links us with our Lord.

What we may find attractive about Peter is his weakness that led him to deny the Lord. That puts him on a level with us. Although it may be comforting to know that someone so distinguished as Peter was a sinner, we also need to appreciate the contribution Peter made by virtue of his leadership and his confession. He continues to stand as a rock along with the other apostles and prophets on whom our Lord builds. We can and should appreciate Peter as the one who pointed to Jesus as the chief cornerstone of the church.

The next day John was there again with two of his disciples. When he saw Jesus passing by, he said, "Look, the Lamb of God!"

When the two disciples heard him say this, they followed Jesus. Turning around, Jesus saw them following and asked, "What do you want?"

They said, "Rabbi" (which means Teacher), "where are you staying?"

"Come," he replied, "and you will see."

So they went and saw where he was staying, and spent that day with him. It was about the tenth hour.

Andrew, Simon Peter's brother, was one of the two who heard what John had said and who had followed Jesus. The first thing Andrew did was to find his brother Simon and tell him, "We have found the Messiah" (that is, the Christ).

Then he brought Simon to Jesus, who looked at him and said, "You are Simon son of John. You will be called Cephas" (which, when translated, is Peter).

John 1:35-42

THREE

ANDREW, THE FIRST EVANGELIST

The disciple Andrew is commonly identified in the Gospels as Peter's brother. This did not seem to bother Andrew. That is notable, for we all know how distressing it can be always to be referred to as "so-and-so's brother." We can sympathize with those young people who do not want to go to the same university as an older brother or sister for fear of being unable to create their own identity. A young man or woman who wants to be something other than an echo of an older brother or sister may feel a strong need to get away from the family image created by someone else.

Perhaps Andrew was secure enough not to be bothered by such second-hand recognition. Maybe family solidarity could have compensated Andrew for always having to take second place. Perhaps Andrew genuinely admired Peter as much as the other disciples did, who accepted him as their leader. At any rate, we have no hint of sibling rivalry between Peter and Andrew. In those few passages that mention Andrew he consistently showed deference to Peter.

Prepared for Discipleship

Andrew lived in the same house with Peter (Mark 1:29) and was a partner in the fishing business with Peter at the Sea of Galilee (Mark 1:16). *Andrew* is a Greek name, and its original form is Andreas, meaning "manly." The brothers came from Bethsaida, an area where people spoke Greek and were acquainted with Greek culture.

In John's gospel Andrew is mentioned as one of the two disciples of Jesus who had a taste of discipleship under John the Baptist. John had called for repentance and announced the dawning of the kingdom of God. He identified Jesus as the Lamb of God, baptized Jesus, and pointed his hearers to him. Andrew was one of two disciples who heard John say, "Behold, the Lamb of God" (John 1:19-36). Andrew was prepared for the arrival of Jesus by the persuasive preaching of John. Later Andrew himself would be a powerful witness to the Lord.

He Followed Jesus

John the Baptist trained Andrew well. No sooner had John pointed to Jesus as the Lamb of God when the two disciples followed Jesus (John 1:37). We can imagine how excitedly Andrew and his companion took out after Jesus once they learned his identity. Their natural curiosity was fed by centuries of messianic expectation by the Jewish people. Now they were only steps away from meeting the Messiah. We can understand their nervous reply when Jesus turned and asked what they were seeking. They simply said, "Rabbi, where are you staying?" (John 1:38).

At that moment they would have been satisfied to know Jesus' address, so that they could hang around and possibly learn a little more about him. However, they received far more than they requested. They were invited to tag along and were also graciously received as guests for the remainder of that day. We can well imagine how that conversation went. Andrew and his friend undoubtedly related how they had been disciples of John and how John had pointed them in the direction of Jesus. No doubt they learned that Jesus was appreciative of John's ministry and that John had not taught them in vain. That afternoon must have been one of the most memorable days of Andrew's life.

He Brought Peter

Andrew did not regard the experience of meeting Jesus as something to be hoarded and treasured only for himself. The first thing Andrew did was to find his brother Simon and tell him, "We have found the Messiah." Then he brought Simon to Jesus. No one had to give Andrew a lesson in evangelism. No one had to convince him that he should go out and share the good news with someone. He immediately went out to tell someone.

Sometimes it is difficult to share the faith with our relatives. Pastors are regularly instructed by families to handle a relative, because members are reticient to talk to their own. They say, "You know he won't listen to us." It is a courageous person who is willing to confront members of the same household. Sometimes we are timid in facing someone near to us because we know our own weaknesses.

It was a self-assured Andrew with faith to share who went to his brother and brought him to Jesus. We do not know which of the brothers was the older of the two. Because Peter emerges as the leader of the apostles, some assume that he was older. However, it is a strong tradition in the eastern churches that Andrew was the older and for that reason was the "first called."

He Offered Help

One of the few other occasions in which we hear from Andrew is at the feeding of the five thousand. At that time Jesus asked how they could buy bread for the multitude. One of the Twelve answered that they did not have enough money in their treasury. Andrew quickly added, "Here is a boy with five small barley loaves and two small fish, but how far will they go among so many?" (John 6:9). Andrew realized that the boy did not have enough for the crowds, but this was something to begin with. Nor did our Lord refuse the offer. Jesus took the boy's offerings, gave thanks for them, and distributed them to the people.

The feeding was to be a sign by which all the people could recognize Jesus as the Messiah. The people did accept the sign, but unfortunately they interpreted it to mean that they could make Jesus a "bread king" who could guarantee them the proverbial free lunch.

In this dramatic scene Andrew paid attention to a young boy. The Andrew who brought his brother to Jesus and permitted him to take first place in the company of our Lord's disciples also permitted a boy to take center stage on that day when Jesus used so little to do so much for so many.

Go-Between

Another incident which gives us some insight into the character of Andrew took place in the week of our Lord's passion at Jerusalem. Some of the worshipers who had come to the holy city to celebrate the Passover spoke Greek. They were curious about Jesus, so they requested an audience with him. Naturally, they approached a disciple with a Greek name who could speak Greek. They said to Philip,

"Sir, we would like to see Jesus" (John 12:21). Philip was not too sure what to do about this, so he conferred with the Greek-speaking Andrew.

Once again, it was the self-assured Andrew who took Philip with him and laid the request before Jesus. Andrew's compassion for people prompted him to action. Whether he was dealing with a brother, a young boy, or people who might have been regarded as lukewarm to the cause of Christ, he brought them all to Jesus.

Although Andrew, the first called, had given first place to his brother, one might have expected to find him in the inner circle of the Lord along with Peter, James, and John. After all, James and John were brothers, too. Yet Jesus did not invite Andrew in on those special occasions. But there was one time when the three included Andrew in a discussion with Jesus about the last days (Mark 13:1-37). No doubt, Andrew relished that moment when he made it with the special group, but there is no sign he ever begrudged the others their special time with Jesus. He was content to be there when he was asked.

There is a popular tradition that Andrew died a martyr at Patras, Greece. He is said to have been tied to a cross in the form of an X, and that he preached from the cross for three days before he died.

An Appreciation

Knowing what we do about human nature, we might expect Andrew to have become bitter for having to live in the shadow of Peter. Instead, Andrew was consistent in his desire to bring people to the Lord. From that first moment when he recognized Jesus as the Lamb of God to the day that he witnessed to the Lord's ascension (Acts 1:13), Andrew knew that he was involved in the life of the Savior of the world.

When Andrew told Peter, "We have found the Messiah," he meant, "We have found the Redeemer, the Savior of the world." In time he would see that Jesus was the Savior through his life, death, and resurrection. Later, his brother Peter was the one who first expressed that faith in words and led the Twelve in getting the word out. But Andrew can be credited with getting all that started, because as the first called he was the first one to share. He is a model for us in the selfless manner in which he evangelized, an example of how one can be oneself, serve quietly, and offer oneself to God. God does the rest.

It was about this time that King Herod arrested some who belonged to the church, intending to persecute them. He had James, the brother of John, put to death with the sword.

Acts 12:1-2

FOUR

JAMES, THE FIRST
APOSTOLIC MARTYR

The disciple James is an intriguing figure because even though we know little about him, in each roster of the Twelve he ranks among the top three. In Mark 3:16 he is listed second. In Matthew 10:2, Luke 6:14, and Acts 1:13 James is named after Peter and Andrew. In addition, James is cited as being a member of the inner circle of three who were with Jesus on special occasions.

Such consistent ranking suggests that James had well-established credentials. Because he was the first of the Twelve to suffer martyrdom, he may have been so highly regarded as to make him second in importance only to Peter.

From Good Stock

James was a brother of another disciple, John. With the exception of one incident, James is never mentioned without John. Because James is mentioned first when the two names are cited, he may have been the older of the two. Like the other set of brothers among the Twelve, Peter and Andrew, James and John were fishermen. Like Peter and Andrew, they were called from their vocation at the sea-shore to become "fishers of men" (Mark 1:16-20). They had worked for their father Zebedee, who was able to carry on his fishing business with his hired servants when James and John left to follow Jesus.

The mother of James and John was one of the women who followed Jesus and was a witness to his crucifixion (Matt. 27:56). Perhaps the mother of James and John was the Salome mentioned by Mark (15:40). Some have sug-gested that a third woman at the cross, mentioned in John 19:25 as the sister of Jesus' mother, was Salome. If that is true, then James and John were Jesus' cousins. What we do know for sure is that James and John came from parents who concurred in their willingness to follow the Lord and apparently were themselves involved in the early Christian movement. James probably found great strength in the fact that his parents were also followers of Christ.

Name and Nickname

The original Hebrew form of James is Jacob, a name treasured in Hebrew tradition because Jacob was the pro-genitor of the 12 tribes of Israel. Because the name was common, there is considerable confusion about the several persons in the company of Jesus with that name. In order to distinguish between some of these, James was dubbed "the Greater," in contrast to James "the Lesser" or "the younger" (Mark 15:40).

The Lord also gave James a special name. He bestowed the name "Boanerges" on James and his brother John, meaning "sons of thunder" (Mark 3:17). Why Jesus gave

them this nickname has been cause for considerable speculation. Some have suggested that James and John were
people of tremendous eloquence with powerful voices. Others have thought that the name described their fiery temperament. Still others, that the name indicates the zeal with
which these men dedicated themselves to the Lord. Perhaps the name is best understood as a means by which Jesus
restrained the enthusiasm of these brothers, which they
revealed on two occasions.

One such incident occurred as Jesus prepared to go to
Jerusalem for his passion. When he and the Twelve were
traveling through Samaria, he sent messengers ahead to
make reservations for them in one of the towns. Because
of the antagonism between the Samaritans and the Jews,
the Samaritans refused them lodging. When James and
John heard that, they said, "Lord, do you want us to call
fire down from heaven to destroy them?" (Luke 9:54). Some
manuscripts add, "as Elijah did." James and John thought
it would be justifiable to act in the spirit of Elijah just before
he was taken to heaven (2 Kings 1:9-15).

The request gives some insight into the confidence James
and John had in Jesus as a messianic figure like Elijah. But
the Lord did not take the request either as a form of flattery
or as an appropriate manner in which to handle the incident. Instead, Jesus "turned and rebuked them" (Luke
9:55). Some manuscripts also add that he said, "You do not
know what kind of spirit you are of, for the Son of Man did
not come to destroy men's lives, but to save them."

His Bold Request

On the way to Jerusalem James and John approached
Jesus with a favor: "Teacher, we want you to do for us
whatever we ask" (Mark 10:35). Jesus replied by asking

them to be specific. They then asked for the privilege to sit on his right and on his left in his glory.

Jesus responded by telling them that they did not know what they were asking. Would they be able to drink from the cup of his suffering or be baptized with the baptism of pain that he would have to endure?

They answered, "We can."

Jesus blessed them for that answer and said that they would indeed. But Jesus also told them that it was not his right to grant their request. That right belonged to his heavenly Father. Jesus did not, however, rule out the possibility that they would achieve their request. He did give the Twelve his rule of greatness, that whoever would be great must be the slave of all (Mark 10:44).

The request of James and John seems audacious and selfish. Mark reports that the other 10 disciples "began to be indignant with James and John" (Mark 10:41). However, we see the whole matter differently when we realize that this request was made after the Lord announced that he was going to Jerusalem for his passion. Then we see the request as a confession of faith on the part of James and an avowed willingness to accept martyrdom for our Lord. That part of the prayer was granted.

His Privilege

James is mentioned as one who was with Jesus in his ministry from the beginning and was included with the Twelve in the Lord's busy rounds (Mark 1:16-39). In addition, James was a part of that inner circle with Peter and John who accompanied Jesus on special occasions. They were present when Jesus raised the daughter of the ruler of the synagogue (Mark 5:35-43). They were privileged to share in the hour of glory when the Lord was transfigured in the mount (Mark 9:2-8).

The trio included Andrew in a discussion with Jesus about the last things as they surveyed the skyline of Jerusalem (Mark 13). On the night in which he was betrayed, Jesus took his trusted three with him into the Garden of Gethsemane to be with him and support him as he prepared for the climax of his passion. The trio had been permitted to behold the vision of the Lord's glory, but they also traversed the valley of the shadow of death with him. They were being prepared for another day.

His Martyrdom

Curiously, John's gospel does not mention the name of James. The story of the Easter breakfast in chapter 21 does say that the sons of Zebedee were present. The suggestion has been offered that the "disciple whom Jesus loved" of the Fourth Gospel could be James, though tradition is heavily weighted on the side of John.

The one incident in which the name of James stands on its own is the brief description of his martyrdom: "It was about this time that Herod the King arrested some who belonged to the church, intending to persecute them. He had James, the brother of John, put to death with the sword" (Acts 12:1-2). We believe that this happened in A.D. 42, under Herod Agrippa. Why Herod did not have Peter beheaded first, since he was the apparent leader, we cannot say. After the martyrdom of James, Herod did have Peter imprisoned, because the death of James appeared to please the populace.

James must have been an important person who shared prominently in the leadership in the Christian movement for about a dozen years. One tradition has it that he carried the gospel to Spain and was martyred at Jerusalem when he returned to report on his mission.

His Legacy

Legends surround the martyrdom of James. One of them claims that the prosecutor who brought James to trial was so impressed by his faith that the official confessed that he also was a Christian. Both of them are said to have been led away together, and the prosecutor begged James' forgiveness. James bestowed peace on the man and kissed him. They were then both beheaded.

James was a person of great faith and forgiveness. His request that he be granted a prominent place in the kingdom must be seen in the light of his willingness to share in the suffering that the Lord had to endure for our sake in his passion and death on the cross. When Jesus questioned whether James understood all that was involved, James answered in the affirmative. James did not make that statement lightly. His commitment was full and complete. He died in a heroic moment as he testified to the faith that the Lord Jesus Christ is truly Savior and Redeemer. Though his career was shorter than that of the other disciples, James' martyrdom helped pave the way for the growth of the church.

We are in his debt for contributing to the spread of the gospel to our time and place. We are also in his debt for being an example to us to give ourselves fully to Jesus' cause, so that in freedom we might also be able to suffer for his sake.

Simon Peter and another disciple were following Jesus.
Because this disciple was known to the high priest, he
went with Jesus into the high priest's courtyard, but
Peter had to wait outside at the door. The other disciple,
who was known to the high priest, came back, spoke to
the girl on duty there, and brought Peter in.

John 18:15-16

FIVE

JOHN, THE QUIET BUT INFLUENTIAL ONE

An interesting sidelight in the history of Jesus' passion is the revelation that an unnamed disciple "was known to the high priest" (John 18:15). What is curious about this information is that it appears so unlikely. None of the disciples was from Jerusalem. There are no other hints that any of the disciples had such contacts, and one would expect a natural tension to exist between the disciples and the high priest, because of the officious attitude of the religious leaders toward Jesus.

William Barclay, a New Testament scholar, uncovered an item he believes might be a clue to that mystery. He learned of a little house in Jerusalem that contains stones and arches that were once a part of a church. According to a Franciscan tradition, the church had been erected on a site which had belonged to Zebedee, the father of James and John. The tradition held that the Zebedee family, who were fish merchants located in Galilee, had a branch market in Jerusalem from which they supplied the family of the high priest. If that were true, it would explain how a disciple was "known to the high priest," and it would also help to identify this disciple as John, the son of Zebedee.

Which John?

This kind of speculation indicates why the identity of John is not simple, even though material about John is plentiful. Tradition ascribes the Fourth Gospel, the Johannine letters, and the book of Revelation to John. In the roster of the disciples Mark 3:17 ranks John third. Matthew 10:2 and Luke 6:14 list him fourth. In Acts 1:13 his name appears second only to that of Peter. The prominence of his name in these rankings is supported by his inclusion in the Lord's inner circle along with Peter and his brother James. In addition, he was a constant companion and important associate of Peter after the resurrection.

Apocryphal material about John also abounds so much that some scholars have suggested that there were as many as three different persons named John. Others have been more willing to fuse the materials into one Johannine figure. The result is a Johannine tradition that is beautiful and meaningful, even if the person of John at times appears elusive.

Most Christians have a warm feeling about John. John is often quoted, because in John's writings are preserved Jesus' longer sayings. The gospel is arranged to illuminate the ministry of Jesus, through whom we have fellowship with the Father.

The Brother of James

The synoptic Gospels—Matthew, Mark, and Luke—offer a portrait of John consistent with their portrayal of James, his brother. They are the sons of Zebedee and his wife Salome. According to the synoptics, James and John acted and served together. They were partners with Peter and Andrew in the fishing business (Luke 5:10) along with their father and his hired servants (Mark 1:20). Along with Peter and Andrew, they were very early called into the discipleship of Jesus (Mark 1:19-20, Matt. 4:21-22). They were a part of that inner circle with Peter that was present on the occasions when Jesus raised the daughter of Jairus (Mark 5:37-43), was transfigured on the mount (Mark 9:2), discussed the last days with them and Andrew (Mark 13), and prayed in the Garden of Gethsemane (Mark 14:37). With James, John earned the title Boanerges, "Sons of Thunder," because of their eagerness to command fire to destroy the inhospitable Samaritans (Luke 9:51-56) and their bold request to sit in seats of authority when Christ came into his glory (Mark 10:35-45).

On one occasion an impudent action is reported about John alone. He informed Jesus that he had restrained a man who had been casting out demons in the name of Jesus. Jesus instructed John to allow the man to do this, and explained that people should develop compassion and demonstrate kindness in his name (Mark 9:38-50). At another time John was with Peter with orders to prepare the Passover for Jesus to eat with the disciples (Luke 22:7-13).

The Disciple Whom Jesus Loved

The name of John is not mentioned in the Fourth Gospel, but there is an unnamed disciple with Andrew who leaves John the Baptist to follow Jesus (1:35-42). There is also a person who is called the disciple "whom Jesus loved" (John 13:23). A long-standing tradition has been challenged by those who have difficulty matching the tempestuous John of the synoptic Gospels with the genteel and loving person of the Fourth Gospel. Also, the suggestion that modesty kept John from using his own name in writing this gospel does not seem convincing in the light of the idealistic picture that is drawn of the disciple whom Jesus loved.

This disciple whom Jesus loved reclined next to Jesus in the upper room, which means that he was probably at his right hand (13:23-25). He was the one who was entrusted with the care of Mary, Jesus' mother, at the cross (John 19:26-27). He was the one who arrived at the empty tomb before Peter on Easter morning (John 20:1-10). It is also a safe assumption that the disciple whom Jesus loved was the unnamed disciple "who was known to the high priest" (John 18:15-16). The most convincing solution to this identity problem is to accept the tradition that this disciple is John, but to recognize that John did not write the Fourth Gospel. Instead, one of John's disciples edited the materials received from John. Such a one could write with admiration about his teacher as "the disciple whom Jesus loved."

John in Acts

What gives credibility to the identification of John as the disciple whom Jesus loved is the account we have of him in the book of Acts. There, too, he is prominent, although none of his speeches are recorded. He was present for the healing of the lame man at the temple (Acts 3:1-10). He was imprisoned along with Peter (Acts 4:1-22). He accompanied Peter in Samaria to follow up on the work of the evangelist Philip (Acts 8:14-25). Back at Jerusalem John must have continued in a leadership role, because the apostle Paul later referred to him as one of the "pillars" of the church (Gal. 2:9). There are no signs of pomposity in this John, no contradiction of the character of the disciple whom

Jesus loved. The quiet but faithful John of Acts is no different from the John of the Fourth Gospel.

Nor is this person different from the John of the synoptic gospels. If we chalk up the daring requests of James and John as immature judgments of willing but faithful and believing disciples, we can readily understand how Jesus could apply the nickname, "Son of Thunder" in a charming way to a disciple whom he loved. Jesus, of course, loved all the disciples. The author of the Fourth Gospel reports that "Jesus knew that the time had come for him to leave this world and go to the Father. Having loved his own who were in the world, he now showed them the full extent of his love" (John 13:1). In his farewell discourse Jesus also said to them all, "As the Father has loved me, so have I loved you" (John 15:9). The title, the "disciple whom Jesus loved," was not meant to be cryptic; it was an honorable way for the author of the Fourth Gospel to refer to his teacher, whom he also loved.

The Aging John

The last chapter of the Fourth Gospel also serves to identify John as the disciple whom Jesus loved. Among those listed as present at the seashore breakfast are the sons of Zebedee (John 21:2). When our Lord absolved and reinstated Peter to his apostolic role, he also indicated that Peter would suffer martyrdom (John 21:19). At that point Peter questioned what the fate would be for the disciple whom Jesus loved. Jesus gave an indirect answer that many interpreted to mean that this disciple would not die (John 21:20-24).

Tradition and legend have it that John did live to a ripe, old age. Because he lived long, pious stories grew up around him, many of them fanciful and obvious fiction. Others are consistent with the loving character portrayed in the New Testament. It is for this reason that the letters which we know as First, Second, and Third John are also ascribed to the disciple John. However, it does not seem John wrote them, because the author identifies himself as "the elder" (2 John 1 and 3 John 1). The style of writing is very much like that of the Fourth Gospel, and the authors of the gospel and the epistles may be one and the same. People ascribed the epistles to the disciple John because of the central message, which is the love of God in Christ Jesus.

Tradition also ascribes the authorship of the book of Revelation to the disciple John. The book is written by someone named John (Rev. 1:1,4). The message of the book is one of comfort and hope for Christians in a time of persecution, and the disciple John lived long enough to witness the widespread kind of persecution of which the book speaks. The name of John the disciple would establish apostolic authority for this writing. However, other considerations make it difficult to establish his authorship of the book with certainty.

The Heart of the Matter

The grave of John was at Ephesus, where a chapel was reared to mark the spot. Later the Emperor Justinian erected a church there that was destroyed by an earthquake. What has remained as an indestructible monument to John, however, has been the tradition that has attributed to him the five writings that have been cherished by the church for the inspiration they have been through the centuries.

One can picture how John may have passed on the material for his gospel to his disciples, and how they cherished his sharing it with them. Today, too, we return to this gospel over and over again for the faith-strengthening power it gives in its witness to the life, death, and resurrection of our Lord Jesus Christ. It is that gospel which contains what Luther called "the gospel in a nutshell": "God so loved the world that he gave his one and only Son, that whoever believes in him shall not perish but have eternal life" (John 3:16). For John, that was the heart of the matter. For him to know Christ was to know God. To know God is to have life eternal (John 17:3). With John we can say, "We have seen his glory" (John 1:14).

The next day Jesus decided to leave for Galilee.
Finding Philip, he said to him, "Follow me."

Philip, like Andrew and Peter, was from the town of
Bethsaida. Philip found Nathanael and told him, "We
have found the one Moses wrote about in the Law, and
about whom the prophets also wrote—Jesus of Nazareth,
the son of Joseph."

"Nazareth! Can anything good come from there?"
Nathanael asked.

"Come and see," said Philip.

John 1:43-46

SIX

PHILIP, THE TIMID ONE

The first one to hear the Lord's gracious invitation, "Follow me," was Philip. According to the Fourth Gospel, John and Andrew, disciples of John the Baptist, were directed by him to Jesus. Andrew then brought his brother Peter to Jesus. On the day following in Galilee, Jesus found Philip and recruited him with a request that was persuasive and compelling. If this had been the only piece of information about Philip we had in the Fourth Gospel, it would have been worthy of notice.

The other three Gospels do little more than mention Philip. However, Matthew 10:3, Mark 3:18, Luke 6:14, and Acts 1:13 rank Philip fifth in the order of the disciples. Such a secure place in the roster of the Twelve suggests that to have been the first one called in this way by Jesus was truly an honor. There is no other scriptural evidence that Philip distinguished himself by dramatic service or by significant insights into the movement Jesus was heading. What we do know about Philip makes him lovable and helps us to empathize with him for expressing some of the feelings that we have as followers of Jesus.

He Knows Greek

Philip's name is Greek and means "lover of horses." He was Hebrew and came from Bethsaida (John 1:44), a city which had been a part of the kingdom of the tetrarch Philip (Mark 6:17), who ruled 4 B.C. to A.D. 34. It was customary in some parts of the world to name children after the ruler, and Philip's parents may have done that. Bethsaida was one of those villages in a territory in which the Hebrews spoke Greek and wanted to identify with Greek culture. To give one's child a popular Greek name may have been one way of witnessing to the fact that Philip's parents did not find the new culture totally incompatible with the messianic hope that they had also imbued in their son.

Philip's hometown is also identified as the town of Peter and Andrew (John 1:44). This may mean that Philip was not only acquainted with Peter and Andrew, but that they were associates of some sort. Perhaps Philip was in the fishing business with Peter and Andrew. Philip may have benefited from his friendship with Peter and Andrew and by sharing the same cultural background. Though Jesus warned that the city of Bethsaida was doomed to judgment (Matt. 11:21), Philip could always say, along with Peter and Andrew, that there they had been prepared for the coming of the Messiah.

Philip the Evangelist

Soon after our Lord had called him, Philip went and found Nathanael. He did not wait for a special occasion to approach his friend. He went directly to Nathanael and said,

"We have found the one Moses wrote about in the Law, and about whom the prophets wrote—Jesus of Nazareth, the son of Joseph" (John 1:45). That was a profound witness for one who had known Jesus only a short time. It seems to show that Philip had a good understanding of Israel's messianic hope, which culminated in the sending of this unique Son.

This confession of Philip identifies the one who was awaited these many centuries as "Jesus of Nazareth, the son of Joseph." Philip did not superimpose on Jesus the many idealized romantic and heroic details of the messianic traditions. Neither was he offended by the ordinary human appearance of Jesus.

Nathanael found Philip's news difficult to accept. "Can anything good come from Nazareth?" Nathanael asked (John 1:46). Philip answered, "Come and see." That was good evangelism. Philip had been convinced in his heart; he invited Nathanael to come and have the same spiritual insight he had. Evangelism does not win by logic or reason. Evangelism leads people to Christ so they can be won by his saving love and grace.

Tested by Jesus

This low-key approach of Philip in evangelizing Nathanael was typical of Philip as he is described in John's gospel. One can be an effective evangelist without being intense and energetic. Many Christians have been of the same temperament as Philip and have done their part effectively for the kingdom.

The timidity of Philip is also obvious when Jesus approached him to ask how they were to buy enough bread to feed the five thousand (John 6:1-7). According to the evangelist, Jesus already knew how he would feed them, but he wanted to test Philip. Why Philip? Perhaps he was in charge of food for the Twelve, or perhaps because they were near Bethsaida, Philip would have known what was available locally. Whatever the reason, Philip answered that eight months' wages would not buy enough bread for the crowd (John 6:7). Apparently Philip figured that if Jesus were to lay this responsibility on the disciples, they would not be able to handle it, and it did not occur to him that he could ask Jesus to do something for the crowd.

Most Christians could identify with Philip's predicament on that occasion. Only one other of the Twelve ventured a suggestion. Andrew brought the young lad who had two fish and five barley loaves, yet Andrew qualified his offering with the question, "But how far will they go among so many?" (John 6:9). Instead of making excuses for Philip, we can admit our weaknesses and realize that our Lord is able to use us in spite of our shortcomings, just as he did Philip.

Approached by Greeks

During Holy Week Philip displayed the same reticence. Some Greeks who had come to celebrate the Passover came to Philip with the request to see Jesus. The Greeks asked this favor of Philip, because his Greek name suggested that he spoke Greek and that he might have an approving attitude toward them. Philip hesitated, however. He apparently was not sure of Jesus' reaction. He took the request to his Greek-speaking friend Andrew, and together they approached Jesus. Once again we can compare this reluctance of Philip with our own cautious attitude at times. We can also give Philip credit for doing what he did. He was not an impediment to a meeting between Jesus and the Greeks, but opened the way by going to one who might be able to do something.

He Searched for the Truth

That Philip learned from his experiences with Jesus is obvious from the last glimpse we have of him in the Fourth Gospel. In his farewell discourse, Jesus comforted the Twelve and prepared them for the way in which he would go to the Father—through his suffering, death, resurrection, and ascension. (John 14).

Thomas reacted by asking about the way Jesus was going. Jesus explained, "I am the way, the truth and the life. No one comes to the Father except through me. If you really knew me, you would know my Father as well. From now on, you do know him and have seen him" (John 14:6-7).

Philip immediately responded, "Lord, show us the Father, and that will be enough for us." For once, Philip asked boldly and without hesitation. He asked well, too. He prayed for what every religious person yearns: we want to see God. Jesus asked Philip if he did not understand that when the disciples had seen Jesus they had seen the Father. The disciples did not really understand this until after Jesus died, rose and ascended to the Father, but Philip's question gave Jesus the opportunity to clarify his identity (John 14:11).

Philip's Later Life

Philip, the disciple of our Lord, is often confused with Philip the evangelist in the book of Acts. That Philip was one of the seven chosen to assist the Twelve (Acts 6:1-6). Philip the evangelist initiated a highly successful missionary enterprise in Samaria (Acts 8:4-17), was instrumental in the conversion of the Ethiopian eunuch (Acts 8:26-40), and hosted Paul in Caesarea (Acts 21:7-10). We can be sure that this Philip was not one of the Twelve, because Peter and John had to go to Samaria to put their blessing on the work of Philip the evangelist. If it had been Philip the apostle, that trip of Peter and John would not have been necessary.

The apostle Philip is mentioned in the book of Acts only as having been present in the upper room (1:13) and again at Pentecost 2:1-7). According to legend, however, Philip traveled to Lydia, Asia, Parthia, and Gaul. Most of the apocryphal stories about Philip are out of character with his person—and with the gospel itself. However, the legends are so consistent in naming Philip as one of the leaders of the Christian movement in Asia that there may be some basis for that in fact.

A Model of Grace

The legends about Philip say that he was martyred at Hierapolis. One tradition maintains that Philip died of natural causes. Another claims that he was crucified. Still another says he was hanged. According to one tradition, Philip asked that after his death he not be wrapped in linen but in papyrus, because he did not feel worthy of the same treatment afforded the Lord at his death. That sounds typical of Philip.

In Philip we see a model for many Christians who are faithful in every way but do not attract much attention. They are those people who can make a quiet and effective witness without being argumentative. They are cautious, and they weigh matters before jumping to conclusions. Open to the gospel and to people, they are warm and gracious. Some of us who are more frenetic in our relationships with each other and with the Lord can learn from Philip's gentleness.

Philip found Nathanael and told him, "We have found the one Moses wrote about in the Law, and about whom the prophets also wrote—Jesus of Nazareth, the son of Joseph."

"Nazareth! Can anything good come from there?" Nathanael asked.

"Come and see," said Philip.

When Jesus saw Nathanael approaching, he said of him, "Here is a true Israelite, in whom there is nothing false."

"How do you know me?" Nathanael asked.

Jesus answered, "I saw you while you were still under the fig tree before Philip called you."

Then Nathanael declared, "Rabbi, you are the Son of God; you are the King of Israel."

Jesus said, "You will believe because I told you I saw you under the fig tree. You shall see greater things than that." He then added, "I tell you the truth, you shall see heaven open, and the angels of God ascending and descending on the Son of Man."

John 1:45-51

SEVEN

BARTHOLOMEW, THE GUILELESS ONE

innocent, naive

Bartholomew's name occurs in every list of the Twelve. He ranks sixth in Matthew 10:3, Mark 3:18, and Luke 6:14, and seventh in Acts 1:13. Apart from his name in these rosters we would know nothing about Bartholomew if we could not identify him with the disciple Nathanael, mentioned in the Fourth Gospel.

Although not all scholars agree, there are several reasons for believing that Bartholomew was Nathanael.

The first is that in the story of the calling of Nathanael it was Philip who brought Nathanael to Jesus. In the other gospels the name of Bartholomew is always mentioned with Philip. This suggests that the two who had been friends before meeting Jesus remained close associates.

A second reason for linking the names of Nathanael and Bartholomew is that the name Bartholomew is a patronymic (derived from the name of the father) for in Hebrew *Bar* means "son." The name is probably "Son of Talmai" (2 Sam. 13:37). Because this was a noble name at the time of Jesus, the three evangelists may have used the patronymic to suggest that there was someone of standing among them. A tholmai was also highly regarded in Hebrew circles as a leader of Scripture study, and Bartholomew may have been an adherent of that school.

A third reason for assuming that Bartholomew and Nathanael are identical is that the evangelist John does not mention the name Bartholomew. He does mention Nathanael twice. The first time is in the calling of Nathanael, a warm and tender story typical of the manner in which John portrays the softer and human side of the disciples. It would be natural for John to speak of Bartholomew on a first-name basis and call him Nathanael.

A Student of Scripture

It is obvious that Nathanael Bartholomew was an intense student of the Scriptures. Philip said to Nathanael, "We have found the one Moses wrote about in the Law, and about whom the prophets also wrote" (John 1:45). This suggests that Philip and Nathanael had studied the Law and the prophets together.

Also in the beautiful story of Nathanael's first encounter with Jesus, our Lord said, "I saw you while you were still under the fig tree before Philip called you" (John 1:48). The fig tree was and continues to be a favorite tree in Israel. It normally grows to about 15 feet in height, with an expanse of branches that affords shade and privacy for meditation. Rabbis and students of the Scriptures thought of the fig tree as a suitable place for their study. According to tradition, when Jesus saw him under the fig tree, Nathanael had been praying for the coming of the Messiah.

Overcoming His Prejudice

That Nathanael Bartholomew was a good student of the Scripture is also signaled by the question he raised for Philip: "Nazareth! Can anything good come from there?" Although this question reveals Bartholomew's prejudice, he was forthright. He openly expressed his doubts in the form of a question.

Nathanael Bartholomew did not allow his prejudice to hinder his acceptance of Philip's invitation. He was willing to open his mind and his heart to the possibility that Philip might be right about this man from Nazareth. The evangelist indicates no interval between the invitation of Philip and the report that Jesus saw Nathanael approaching (John 1:46-47). That meant Nathanael did not mull over the offer of Philip. He did not ask Philip to offer proofs for his conviction about Jesus. He valued his friend and responded to his good word.

Whatever skepticism still lingered in Nathanael's heart was swept away by the reception he received from Jesus. As he was still approaching, Jesus said, "Here is a true Israelite, in whom there is nothing false" (John 1:47). Nathanael must have been overwhelmed by this tribute. Jesus did not intend to say that Nathanael was without sin, but that he was a person of high integrity, sincerity, and commitment to God.

Perhaps embarrassed by Jesus' compliment, Nathanael asked, "How do you know me?" (John 1:48). When Jesus answered that he had seen Nathanael before Philip called him and while he was meditating under the fig tree, he was referring to the transparent character of Nathanael. A person who had been singled out because of dedication to God had nothing to hide. Jesus was the one of whom the evangelist could say, "He did not need man's testimony about man, for he knew what was in a man" (John 2:24).

Nathanael experienced Jesus' ability to see through people. That was enough for him. He replied, "Rabbi, you are the Son of God; you are the King of Israel" (John 1:49). All doubts were swept aside for Nathanael, and he immediately broke into a beautiful confession of faith, incorporating two of the most noble messianic titles: Son of God and King of Israel.

Nathanael thus proved that Jesus' estimate of him was true. Nathanael knew he could entrust himself in faith to one who understood how deeply he yearned for God. Such a one had to be the Messiah.

Greater Things Promised

This introductory meeting with Jesus had to produce sheer joy in the heart of Nathanael Bartholomew. It was also the harbinger of greater things to come. Jesus said to Nathanael, "You believe because I told you I saw you under the fig tree. You shall see greater things than that. . . . You shall see the heaven open, and the angels of God ascending and descending on the Son of Man" (John 1:50-51). Jesus promised this guileless Israelite that the vision of Jacob (or Israel) at Bethel would be repeated for him. Jesus was to be the fulfillment of the dream of Israel. The angels of God ascended and descended on him in his ministry and at his suffering, death, resurrection, and ascension.

Nathanael Bartholomew was witness to all of that. He was present at the Easter breakfast at the seashore (John 21:1-14) to celebrate the fact that the one whom he confessed as King of Israel had emerged victorious from the cross that had been labeled, "Jesus of Nazareth, the King of the Jews." Bartholomew was present at the upper room when the disciples returned from that breath-taking sight of the Lord's ascension (Acts 1:12-14).

After that, legends about Bartholomew are numerous. He is reported to have preached in India, Phrygia, and Armenia. Tradition has it that he founded the church in Armenia and that he was martyred there, but another legend locates his martyrdom in India.

An Ideal for Us

The story of the calling of Nathanael Bartholomew reveals the warmth, grace, and kindness of Jesus. It also reflects the naivete, the innocence, and the purity of heart of Nathanael Bartholomew.

What was true of Bartholomew is characteristic of all who would follow after our Lord: we are incomplete without Jesus. No matter how pious, pure of heart, or dedicated we are, our prejudices, biases, or some other flaw will betray us as imperfect and corrupted by sin. As Nathanael Bartholomew discovered, Jesus of Nazareth can free us from our sin. We can be open with him, ourselves, and God and admit the imperfection within us.

Through Christ we also attain to our vision of God and heaven as by faith we participate in his death and resurrection.

As Jesus went on from there, he saw a man named Matthew sitting at the tax collector's booth. "Follow me," he told him, and Matthew got up and followed him.

While Jesus was having dinner at Matthew's house, many tax collectors and "sinners" came and ate with him and his disciples.

Matthew 9:9-10

EIGHT

MATTHEW, THE TAX COLLECTOR

It is said that nothing is certain in life—except death and taxes. Neither one is a favorite topic for conversation, yet we cannot stop talking about them. Although taxes are the subject of endless national debates, government officials try to avoid the topic in election years, because they do not want to be identified as the ones who levied taxes.

In Jesus' day, taxes were not popular either, especially because they had to be paid to an alien government. The Jewish people did not like being enslaved to Rome. Although at various points in their history they had been a vassal state and had been in captivity, they maintained a sense of freedom and boasted, "We are Abraham's descendants and have never been slaves of anyone" (John 8:33).

Jewish antagonism against paying taxes to maintain a foreign military establishment in their own land was deepened when they paid these taxes to fellow Jews who were willing

to collect on behalf of the Roman Empire. These tax collectors were seen as traitors who had betrayed both God
and country. It was no wonder, then, that Jesus created a
stir when he chose one of them to be his disciple.

Called on the Job

The gospel of Matthew identifies the tax collector whom
Jesus called as Matthew (9:9). Mark 2:14 and Luke 5:27
name the person Levi. Mark adds that he was as the "son
of Alphaeus," an identification which the Gospels otherwise
reserve for James the younger. Not all the church fathers
identified Matthew with Levi, yet it appears to be reason-
able and a sound judgment, because Matthew is listed in
the roster of the disciples in Matthew 10:3, Mark 3:18, and
Luke 6:15. In the gospel of Matthew he is also identified
as the tax collector.

Because the identification of Matthew as Levi is fairly
certain, we can assume that Matthew was serving in a tax
collector's booth near Capernaum, in the area where Jesus
regularly traveled. One day Jesus saw him sitting there,
and he said to him, "Follow me." Matthew rose and followed
him (Matt. 9:9). We have no hint as to who noticed whom
first. Nor do we have any idea as to whether they had seen
one another before that day. What we do know is that the
Lord called Matthew. Out of his grace and love he extended
the invitation for Matthew to follow him. The initiative for
discipleship came from Jesus.

The account of the calling of Matthew is so abrupt that
we might think there must have been more to it than that.
Surely there must have been some kind of conversation.
Matthew must have asked what the conditions would be.
Maybe there had been some contacts through friends, we
might think, or perhaps Matthew conveyed the message

that he was interested in following Jesus. The Gospels, however, give no hint of this. They simply state that Matthew was called by the Lord. Matthew was on the job, carrying on the work of his profession, when Jesus came to him.

The call of Matthew echoes the manner in which God called the Old Testament prophets. They were the ones to whom "the word of the Lord came" (Jer. 1:4). To the disciples, the word of the Lord came in the person of Jesus of Nazareth. None of them had special qualifications to be disciples. The call alone qualified them to be what the Lord was to shape them to be in his love and grace. All of them drew the hoots and the jeers of the religious community for their lack of credentials. Matthew was a special target for ridicule, because he was a tax collector, included with the dregs of society, with "sinners" like prostitutes, alcoholics, and other social outcasts.

Public Reaction

The public reaction to the calling of Matthew illustrates the love and grace with which Jesus touched the lives of people. The Lord's acceptance of Matthew was occasion for many tax collectors and "sinners" to come and eat with Jesus and his disciples (Matt. 9:10). If Jesus could remove the social barriers and reach down to the lower strata of society for a disciple, then the call of Matthew was also a call that others could respond to with hearty enthusiasm. Jesus had made a powerful statement to the community when he took Matthew into the circle of his disciples.

Others, also, immediately caught the impact of this strategy. When the Pharisees saw this, they asked his disciples, "Why does your teacher eat with tax collectors and 'sinners'?" (Matt. 9:11). The Pharisees mocked the disciples as unlettered people, but then implied that they should correct their teacher. Jesus himself gave the Pharisees a straightforward answer: "It is not the healthy who need a doctor, but the sick. But go and learn what this means: 'I desire mercy, not sacrifice.' For I have not come to call the righteous, but sinners" (Matt. 9:12-13). When Jesus called him, Matthew was a living sign that all sinners are welcome in our Lord's kingdom.

A Modest Personality

Luke records that the tax collector who was called made a great feast for Jesus in his house (5:29). The banquet was designed to celebrate the calling of the tax collector. The fact that Luke mentions that it was the tax collector who gave the dinner, and the gospel of Matthew simply mentions that while they were at table the other tax collectors and sinners came, gives us some indication of the modesty of Matthew. The same is true about the use of the names. Mark and Luke both identify the tax collector as Levi, but list the disciple as Matthew. It could be they did so out of deference to the disciple Matthew. They used his former name so that his original occupation could be forgotten. Levi could have taken the name Matthew, a Greek form of a common Hebrew name, when he became a follower of Jesus. That would explain why three Gospels list Matthew as a disciple with no mention of Levi (Matt. 10:3; Mark 3:18; Luke 6:15).

Another clue to the personality of Matthew is that in the roster of the disciples in the gospel of Matthew he is also identified as the tax collector. That would indicate that Matthew did not want to forget the magnanimous grace with which Jesus had called him from his former way of life.

The Gospel of Matthew

Other than these few surmises we can make about Matthew, there are no other incidents about him recorded in the Gospels. Of course, the Gospel According to Matthew has been attributed to him by a long-standing tradition. Although not all scholars agree, strong arguments favor this view. One is that the tradition is strong in the early church fathers. More importantly, who among all the disciples was better qualified to write an account of the ministry of Jesus? He was probably the most well-educated, the wealthiest, and the most sophisticated of the Twelve, because of his profession. It seems credible that in his old age Matthew would amplify the Gospel According to Mark. Mark was written to give a quick view of the Lord's ministry. Matthew could have taken the same material and arranged it to include some of Jesus' great discourses and to demonstrate how the Lord's mission was a fulfillment of the Hebrew covenant.

Matthew arranged his Gospel to give a clear picture of the kingly rule of God and the manner in which we are to live under God as his disciples today. In the first four chapters of the Gospel, Matthew sets the stage for the ministry of Jesus with the listing of a genealogy, an infancy narrative, the baptism of Jesus as the Son of God, and the temptations in the wilderness. It would be a tax official and an accountant like Matthew who would ingeniously arrange the genealogy in three groups of fourteen to demonstrate that Jesus was to begin a new generation of believers as the seventh seven. Matthew also arranged his gospel to parallel the great salvation events in Hebrew history.

In addition, Matthew arranged the teachings of Jesus around five major discourses to suggest a pentateuch like the five books of Moses. They are: the Sermon on the Mount

(Matthew 5–7); Instructions in Discipleship (Chap. 10); a collection of Parables (Chap. 13); Discipline in the Kingdom (Chap. 18); and a Discourse on the Last Things (Chaps. 24–25). These teachings, woven through the story of Jesus' ministry, help to interpret his passion, death, and resurrection. Matthew's gospel helps us understand how God fulfilled his promises to the Hebrew people by sending Jesus of Nazareth to be the redeemer of the world.

Traditions about how Matthew carried this gospel as a missionary at various parts of the world are many. The most popular tradition is that he carried the gospel to Ethiopia. The accounts of his martyr's death are so fanciful as to leave us only with the clear impression that he died for the sake of the gospel.

Matthew's Good News for Us

Matthew is an outstanding example of the way our Lord is able to change lives. Matthew promptly answered the dramatic call away from the tax table to follow Jesus, because in the call Jesus offered him the opportunity to accept his love. In answering the call Matthew did not gain acceptance from all other people. If they had hated him for being a tax collector, some continued to despise him for being a disciple of Jesus. Yet he gained acceptance, absolution, peace, and purpose for life from God's Son.

That is what we all basically search for. If we look to our vocation to provide meaning in our lives, eventually we will become disillusioned. What we need is to have our total lives redeemed. Our vocations will of themselves never bring fulfillment for us. That we gain through our Lord's gracious calling.

Matthew understood that. When he gave up his tax table, he gained his life. His account of Jesus' passion reveals how deeply he felt that the ultimate victory was in the one who died and rose again. When our Lord comes to us in the midst of our vocations, we do not have to hold back anything in responding to him, because no matter what it costs us, we gain everything.

Thomas said to him, "Lord, we don't know where you are going, so how can we know the way?"

Jesus said to him, "I am the way and the truth and the life. No one comes to the Father except through me. If you really knew me, you would know my Father as well. From now on, you do know him and have seen him."

John 14:5-7

NINE

THOMAS, THE PESSIMIST

We use the term "doubting Thomas" to describe someone who has serious doubts when the person should feel secure or confident. We do not use that phrase of someone who has an exploring mind that raises the right kind of questions or applies the scientific method in pursuing the truth. This adverse use of the term is unfair to the disciple Thomas, who asked for definite proof of the Lord's resurrection. Furthermore, such a negative view of Thomas singles him out from all of the rest of the disciples, who had an equally difficult time believing that Jesus was risen from the dead. Not only is Thomas representative of our own doubts in the face of the great truths of the gospel, but by his bold curiosity he raised questions that serve the interests of us all.

Called a Twin

What we know about Thomas is somewhat clouded by the fact that we are not sure about his name. The Hebrew name Thomas means "twin"; the Greek equivalent is Didymus. In Hebrew circles there is no record of that as a first name, although there are some instances of its use as a first name in Greek society. There have been a variety of guesses as to who might be the twin of Thomas. Some have suggested that it was Matthew, because Matthew's name is coupled with Thomas in the rosters of the disciples (Matt. 10:3; Mark 3:18; Luke 6:15). One tradition maintains that Thomas was the twin of a sister named Lysia.

One scholar has suggested that the name Thomas is symbolic of the double-mindedness of the man who hovered between belief and unbelief (James 1:8). A Syriac tradition calls him Judas Thomas, or Judas the Twin. The name Thomas was probably used in the circle of the disciples to distinguish him from the other two disciples by the same name. The first three gospels are silent about the personality of Thomas. The Fourth Gospel, however, shares some precious insights into this disciple.

Loyal Disciple

John's gospel portrays Thomas as a devoted and loyal disciple. Thomas did tend to be pessimistic. He also revealed a narrow view of the major issues he confronted as a disciple of Jesus.

When Mary and Martha sent word to Jesus about the illness of Lazarus, Jesus at first delayed going to Bethany in response to their request (John 11:3-6). At the right time, Jesus announced that he was going to the home of his friends. The disciples protested, because they were aware that the tension between Jesus and his enemies was so great that people in Judea would probably stone him. Jesus said he was going to wake Lazarus. The disciples thought that was a sign that Lazarus was recovering. Jesus explained that

Lazarus was dead and that what Jesus was going to do would help them to believe.

Thomas apparently missed the point of the conversation. Perhaps he was concentrating on the risk Jesus was taking by going into Judea and understood how resolute Jesus was in making that trip to see his friend. Thomas blurted out, "Let us also go, that we may die with him" (John 11:16). That was a genuine display of courage and loyalty. Though Thomas missed the larger implication of what Jesus was saying, we have no evidence that the other disciples recognized what Jesus was going to do. In spite of his pessimism, Thomas confessed that Jesus was a leader worth following to the death.

Raising the Right Questions

Not much later, in the Upper Room in which he celebrated the Passover with his disciples, Jesus attempted to prepare his friends for his death, resurrection, and ascension. In a comforting phrase Jesus described his leaving the Twelve as his "going to prepare a place" for them. At that moment he was bringing to a conclusion all that he had shared with his disciples over the years. The culmination of what he had to say to them was that they had nothing to fear, in spite of what they might see in the next hours. Nor were they to be concerned when he would be gone from them, because he would return to take them to himself. Finally, he said, "You know the way to the place where I am going" (John 14:4). This had been the whole purpose of Jesus' mission and ministry which they had shared so intimately.

Thomas, however, reacted as though he had understood nothing of what had gone on. He said, "Lord, we don't know where you are going, so how can we know the way?"

(John 14:5). Once again, Thomas exemplified the incredulity of the Twelve, who could not fathom the manner in which Jesus would work out the fullness of salvation. At that moment they were no more prepared to understand that Jesus would rise from the dead than they were to see Jesus raise Lazarus. Even if it was out of his pessimism that Thomas asked the question, we have to credit him for a beautiful answer from our Lord: "I am the way and the truth and the life. No one comes to the Father except through me" (John 14:6).

The next scene in which we meet Thomas is a week after Easter. He had not been present when the risen Christ appeared to the disciples at their hiding place. On that occasion Jesus not only delighted the disciples with his risen and glorified presence, but he conferred his Spirit on them and gave them the authority to forgive and retain sins. In the Fourth Gospel this appears to have the same apostolic authority that was granted at Pentecost. When Thomas returned to the circle of the disciples, they informed him that they had seen the Lord (John 20:25). Thomas permitted a streak of skepticism to shine through: "Unless I see the nail marks in his hands and put my finger where the nails were, and put my hand in his side, I will not believe it."

Not only does that sound normal for the Thomas we have already met, it is the kind of response we could expect from almost anyone. We live in a world in which death rules tyrannically. It is not at all surprising that Thomas required the signs of death in the nail prints before he could believe that Jesus was alive.

A Great Confession

Jesus did not disappoint Thomas. The following week he appeared to the disciples when Thomas was present. He accommodated Thomas by permitting him to touch the very nail prints he had inquired about. There was no need. Thomas was overwhelmed by the presence of the risen Christ. He confessed, "My Lord and my God!" (John 20:28). That is one of the best confessions in the Scriptures. It is not only a tribute to our Lord, but it also embraces him in faith as the one who makes a claim on our lives because of what he has done for us.

Yet Thomas received no word of commendation from the Lord. Instead, Jesus said, "Because you have seen me you have believed" (John 20:29). Then he offered the highest commendation for those who do not have the benefit of physical evidence: "Blessed are those who have not seen and yet have believed."

Once again, Thomas played an important role clarifying what our Lord was accomplishing for us. The natural pessimism Thomas expressed in his doubts was no impediment to his faith. His natural inclinations became the occasions for faith when he was confronted by Jesus. Thomas contradicted the notion that the disciples had to turn off their brains in order to be Jesus' followers. Along with the others, Thomas gave ample evidence that they were not dim-witted and dull. They were people of integrity who struggled with faith and had to be won by nothing less than the power of God's Spirit.

A Legend in India

Thomas is listed as one of those present for the Easter breakfast recorded in John 21. In Acts 1:13 he is listed as present in the Upper Room. Thomas was also present for the outpouring of the Holy Spirit on Pentecost (Acts 2:1).

Tradition ascribes missionary activity to Thomas in Parthia and India. His reputed burial sites range from a cathedral in Madras, India, to a place in Mesopotamia.

Patron of Doubters

Thomas is the patron saint for anyone who has entertained doubts about the faith or has felt the need to question where the faith is going to lead us. He is also a model of bravery and fidelity. Often we are exposed to people who represent Christianity as a religion for the gullible, submissive, and stupid, but Thomas made it clear that questioning is a part of believing.

In questioning Jesus, Thomas discovered that faith in the Lord is not unreasonable. He learned that what Jesus accomplished by his death and resurrection has completely reversed what we believe about life and death. Death no longer rules us. The risen Christ is now our Lord and our God. In him we find the way, the truth, and the life.

Thomas emerges from the Twelve as one whom we can appreciate and cherish because he asked the right questions. From Thomas we learn that we, too, can raise all the questions we like. Our questions are signs that we take the mission and ministry of our Lord seriously. What our Savior accomplished for us will stand up to all our curiosity, and in the process our faith will be enhanced.

Some women were watching from a distance. Among them were Mary Magdalene, Mary the mother of James the younger and of Joses, and Salome.

Mark 15:40

TEN

JAMES THE YOUNGER

The disciple listed ninth in all four rosters of the Twelve is James, the son of Alphaeus (Matt. 10:3; Mark 3:18; Luke 6:15; Acts 1:13). In the gospel of Mark, he is also identified as the "younger" (Mark 15:40). He is sometimes referred to as "James the Lesser." The Greek word *mikros* could mean that he was "small" (in stature), or the word could have been used to distinguish him from the other disciple James, who was older. The word could also be employed to imply that this James was considered to be less important than James the son of Zebedee, who had been a part of the Lord's inner circle. The term was used that way to designate people who were more modest or less prominent than others. Since Jesus had settled the question about ambition in the kingdom and who was to be considered greater or lesser (Mark 10:35-45), it seems more likely that we should think of this James as the "shorter" or the "younger" of the two disciples who bore that name.

Which James?

We know next to nothing about this James, and there is considerable confusion about his identity, because there were others in the Lord's company with the same name, in addition to James, the son of Zebedee and brother of John. The name James was popular among the Jews, because the Hebrew form of the name is Jacob.

The person most often confused with James the Younger is James the brother of the Lord. During the time the Twelve were with Jesus, James the brother of the Lord was not a follower of Jesus (John 7:5). He became a believer after the resurrection (1 Cor. 15:7) and still later the presiding officer of the Council of Jerusalem (Acts 15:13). Another James mentioned in the lists of those who touched the circle of Jesus' friends and associates was the father of Judas, who was not Judas Iscariot (Luke 6:16).

We have to content ourselves with the fact that we cannot ascribe anything more to James, the son of Alphaeus, than this tidbit of information about his height, or lack of it, or the contrast of his age with that of the other James. However, that does not prevent us from making some observations about him. The mention of his name in the list of those whom the Lord chose makes him important.

The fact that James the Younger is identified as the son of Alphaeus raises some interesting possibilities about his family. Mark—but only Mark—mentions that Levi, whom we identified as Matthew, was also the son of Alphaeus (Mark 2:14). Since the other Gospels do not mention this, and none of them identify Matthew and James as brothers (as they do the other two sets of brothers in the Twelve), it is conceivable that this is a gloss, or addition, to the text. If, on the other hand, Matthew and James were both sons of Alphaeus, some have suggested that James probably was a tax collector like Matthew, but this is only speculation.

However, the text that identifies James as "the Younger" (Mark 15:40) also names Joses as his brother. While Joses was not one of the Twelve, his name is mentioned as one who would have been known to people in the early community of Christians. It is impossible to say how Alphaeus felt about Jesus. However, if he was the father of two or all three of these followers of Jesus, we have to conclude that he had done a good job of raising his children. He had helped to prepare candidates for this school of disciples attached to Jesus. That is an excellent example of the fact that though parents cannot believe for their children, they are God's instrument in helping children become prepared for the operation of God's grace in their lives.

His Faithful Mother

How intimately the family of James the Younger was involved in the circle of the friends and relatives of Jesus is suggested also by the fact that his mother is named as one of those standing by while the Lord was crucified. These were the same women who had ministered to Jesus during his Galilean ministry (Mark 15:40-41). Some church fathers identified this Mary with Mary, wife of Clopas, named in John 19:25. That would make Clopas the same person as Alphaeus, who, some say, was a brother of Joseph of Nazareth. Mary, the wife of Clopas, is also named as the sister of Mary, the mother of the Lord. That hardly seems likely, since a family probably would not give the same name to two daughters. More likely, John is telling us that they were sisters-in-law. Also, Mary the wife of Clopas, and Mary the mother of both James the Younger and Joses probably are not the same person, because there is no ground for identifying the name Clopas with Alphaeus.

Others have tried to identify James the Younger and Joses as Jesus' brothers. When Jesus preached in the synagogue at Nazareth, the people wondered, "Isn't this the carpenter? Isn't this Mary's son and the brother of James, Joses, Judas and Simon? Aren't his sisters here with us?" (Mark 6:3). Mark's description of Mary the mother of James the Younger and Joses, however, distinguishes her from Mary the mother of the Lord.

It is best for us to abandon these strained efforts to make James the Younger related to Jesus' family through his mother. It is sufficient to recognize the important role his mother played in the guild of women who served Jesus at an important time in his ministry. Her faithful service led her all the way to the cross. She also assisted with the burial of Jesus (Mark 15:47) and returned to the tomb early Easter morning (Mark 16:1).

Hidden Service

The attempts to make James the Younger a blood relative of Jesus, either a brother or a cousin, seem to have grown from the need to account for his presence among the disciples. There is no record of Jesus calling James the Younger into his company, other than the general commission cited in the Gospels (Matt. 10:1-42; Mark 3:13-19; Luke 6:13-16). If the church fathers could establish that James the Younger was a close relative of Jesus, they could account for his presence as one who came into the group by virtue of his proximity to Jesus. Furthermore, one could then interpret the silence about James the Younger as the result of his importance as a relative of Jesus.

Such speculation is unnecessary. What is important is that James the Younger, the son of Alphaeus, is included in the group of Twelve as one called by Jesus. James was not called because of his merit, either by his bloodline or by something that he had done. The fact that there is not one recorded deed done or word spoken by James the Younger reminds us that none of these people had earned a place among the Lord's disciples.

The fact that nothing is recorded about James the Younger does not mean he did not play an important role in Jesus' mission and ministry. We know that he responded to the call, that he went out with the Twelve, that he remained in the service of the Lord all the way through the crucifixion, death, resurrection, and ascension. He was present in Jerusalem after the ascension (Acts 1:13; 2:1). It is doubtful that he could have remained in that group through all of that simply as a hanger-on.

More than likely, James the Younger was one of those quiet individuals who make their contributions without a lot of fanfare. He may have been one who did not speak out and did not voice an opinion or offer any kind of challenge. Yet he may have quietly supported the ministry of evangelism and teaching in a variety of ways. He could have run countless errands that were essential and supportive. He could have been one of those who counseled wisely through their active listening. He could have been a meditative and thoughtful person, an effective leader in life of the early church. He could have been one of those imaginative and creative persons who stimulate others into activity by their quiet suggestions. He could have been one of those charitable individuals who give of their possessions and self anonymously and unselfishly.

A Model for Discipleship

We all know believing Christians who fill these kinds of roles in our congregations. They are the people whose names do not get into the church bulletins or into the congregational newsletters. Some of them would be embarrassed to have their names mentioned. Some of them are so regular in their church attendance that if they are not present on Sunday morning, the pastor feels compelled to call on them to see if they are ill. Some are devoted to a life of prayer on behalf of those in need in the congregation and for the larger needs of the world. Some of them carry hot dishes to families bereaved of loved ones or which lack the services of a hospitalized mother or father.

Yet none of these people will be the headliners at an awards night dinner. Nor are they even likely to get honorable mention. Yet none will ever be able to measure the extent of their contribution. In that sense James the Younger is a model for them. We do not know what he contributed to the mission and ministry that was committed to the Twelve. Yet we know that he was a part of it all the way.

What we can sift from the legends about James the Younger is that he was martyred in the cause of the Lord after a life of devotion and service. In that regard he fits into the larger picture of the Twelve, who had been molded into an effective team of witnesses. James was as much a link in the chain of those who preserved that record as any other among the Twelve.

Then Judas (not Iscariot) said to him, "But, Lord, why do you intend to show yourself to us and not to the world?"

Jesus replied, "If anyone loves me, he will obey my teaching. My Father will love him, and we will come to him and make our home with him."

John 14:22-23

ELEVEN

THADDAEUS, NOT JUDAS ISCARIOT

The tenth disciple listed in two rosters of the Twelve (Matt. 13:3 and Mark 3:18) is Thaddaeus. Luke lists him eleventh as Judas, the son of James (Luke 6:16 and Acts 1:13). In some manuscripts of the Matthew text he is Lebbaeus or "Labbaeus called Thaddaeus" (Matt. 10:3).

At first the use of three names for one disciple may appear quite confusing to us. In reality, however, the several names were probably used to avoid confusion. All of us know people who go by their middle names, surnames, or nicknames, by initials, or by designation as a junior to avoid being confused with persons with similar names. The disciples did the same. The names that appear in the rosters of disciples were those by which they were best known in their own circle and in the early Christian community.

That was especially true of Thaddaeus, whose proper name was Judas. The evangelists were careful to distinguish Thaddaeus from Judas Iscariot, because they did not want him to be confused with the disciple who betrayed Jesus.

We can readily appreciate why the evangelists took great pains to disassociate the name of one of the faithful disciples from that of Judas Iscariot. However, we should also note that the name Judas was popular in Hebrew families. The name undoubtedly is associated with the name of Judah, one of the tribes of Israel, named after the son of Israel who was blessed with the messianic promise. In Hebrew the name means "Jahweh leads" or "Jahweh is first." The name also had become legendary because of the folk hero Judas Maccabaeus, who had led a Jewish revolt against Syria.

Judas was also the name of one of Jesus' brothers (Matt. 13:55; Mark 6:3), who was not a follower of Jesus during his ministry. These brothers had actually been antagonistic toward Jesus (John 7:5) and did not become believers until after the resurrection (Acts 1:14). Later they were apparently very active in the missionary enterprise of the young church (1 Cor. 9:5).

One could cite the names of other important figures who had given the name Judas great prominence. However, the concern of the evangelists was simply to make clear that this Judas was "not Iscariot." He was a person with integrity who served faithfully the mission and ministry of our Lord.

His Surnames

The alternate names given to Judas elicit some curiosity as to what was intended by the names. Thaddaeus is a Greek form of a Hebrew word which means "breast." Lebbaeus, the name listed in Matt. 10:3 in some manuscripts, is taken from the Hebrew word *leb*, which means "heart." Both of these names suggest rather endearing terms to describe Judas. It could be that his family had given him the nicknames when he was a child to suggest that he was "all heart," either in the display of his courage or his tenderhearted-ness. It is more likely that the disciples awarded these names to Judas when they observed how consistently tenderhearted or courageous he was in public. Perhaps they used this affectionate title to make the contrast between him and Judas Iscariot. This play on names gives us one small insight into the human side of the disciples.

An Important Question

The evangelist John deepens our insight into the person of Thaddaeus. John records one question that Thaddaeus asked Jesus. The setting was in the Upper Room, where the Lord was trying to prepare the disciples for his imminent crucifixion, resurrection, and ascension. He told them, "Before long, the world will not see me anymore, but you will see me. Because I live, you also will live" (John 14:19).

That raised the serious question in the heart of Thaddaeus, "But, Lord, why do you intend to show yourself to us and not to the world?" (John 14:22).

Some who profess to be Christians are only too happy to think that they will be saved, while countless others will be damned. They hold judgmental attitudes toward unbelievers. They can enumerate endless reasons why the majority of the world should be condemned. However, every thoughtful Christian who understands that we are saved only by the grace and mercy of God in Jesus Christ has to think through this question of Thaddaeus. Why is it that we are saved and not others? That poses profound theological questions that have divided theologians of great acumen. In the case of Thaddaeus, the question was being asked by a grateful believer who expressed enormous sympathy for the plight of the world that does not know Christ as Lord and Savior.

An Important Answer

Thaddaeus' question came from a tender heart, and the response was equally gracious. Jesus replied, "If anyone loves me, he will obey my teaching. My Father will love him, and we will come to him and make our home with him. He who does not love me will not obey my teaching. These words you hear are not my own; they belong to the Father who sent me" (John 14:23-24). God has made a generous offer to the world. In Christ God's love for the world was made manifest. The Father will come to abide with those who accept this love.

Those who cannot believe or accept this offer of love are left to their own devices, doomed to rely on their own self-love, self-hate, the emptiness of their own hearts. They are damned by their own unbelief and failure to trust God. God loves the world in Christ, but God does not force people to love him in return. If they prefer to remain unloved, that has been their own decision.

Jesus' answer no doubt remained something of a mystery to Thaddaeus and the other disciples. They were unable to fathom the depths of this saying until after Jesus was crucified and raised from the dead. Even after the resurrection and ascension, they were still unclear as to what it all meant. At Pentecost they were awakened by God's Spirit to all that God accomplished in the ministry, death, and resurrection of Christ. Jesus promised it would be that way: "All this I have spoken to you while still with you. But the Counselor, the Holy Spirit, whom the Father will send in my name, will teach you all things and will remind you of everything I have said to you" (John 14:25-26).

Remembered in Legends

Tradition has it that Thaddaeus carried the gospel to Edessa and Armenia, where, it is said, he was martyred. In Armenia his name was linked with Simon the Zealot, another of the disciples. The diversity of legends about the missionary activity of Thaddaeus leads us to conclude that all we can say is that Thaddaeus was faithful to the commission given the Twelve, even to the point of death.

How We Can Remember Him

While we cannot speak with certainty about the post-Pentecost activity of Thaddaeus, we do have a legacy from him of profound importance in the one question he is reported to have asked Jesus. From his nickname and from his question, though, we can surmise that he was a person with a gentle spirit. His concern for the world reflected his gratitude for his own salvation by God's grace.

Our own witness, evangelism, and concern for the missionary enterprise of the church grows out of the same kind of compassion. We feel the comforting and reassuring knowledge that we are a part of God's family and that our Lord has been revealed to us. At the same time we feel compassion for those who do not know Christ. This motivates us to get the word out so that others may have the saving knowledge of God in Christ Jesus. That is the proper way for us to show the same heart as Thaddaeus.

When morning came, he called his disciples to him and chose . . . Simon who was called the Zealot.

Luke 6:13-15

TWELVE

SIMON THE ZEALOT

Simon the Zealot is listed tenth in the rosters of Matthew (10:4) and Mark (3:18) and eleventh in Luke 6:15 and in Acts 1:13. The apostles identified Simon as a Zealot to distinguish him from Simon Peter, Andrew's brother, and from one of the brothers of our Lord who also was called Simon (Mark 6:3).

Beyond this identification of him as a Zealot we have no information about Simon. However, we do have information about the Zealot movement, so we can surmise what kind of persons joined its ranks. The inclusion of Simon in the company of the Lord also furnishes additional insight into the nature of the group Jesus called into his service and to whom he entrusted the gospel of reconciliation.

The Zealot Movement

Zealotism developed in Israel after the Exile. The word Zealot comes from a Hebrew root meaning "jealousy." Simeon and Levi, the sons of Jacob, were the prototypes of zealous behavior on behalf of God's people. They slew the men of Shechem and plundered the city, seeking revenge for the rape of their sister Dinah (Gen. 34:25-29). Phineas, a priest and grandson of Aaron, was another heroic figure for the Zealots. Phineas received approbation for his emulation of God's jealousy when he slew a Hebrew who had taken a Midianite woman (Num. 25:10-13). Elijah, the prophet in the Northern Kingdom, was also an example of zeal when he ordered all the prophets of Baal slain (1 Kings 18:39-40). The apostle Paul confessed that before his conversion he had been "extremely zealous" for the tradition of his fathers (Gal. 1:14), as was evidenced by his determination to exterminate all believers in Christ. Even Jesus was referred to as being zealous when he drove the money changers from the temple (John 2:17).

The Zealotic movement was inspired by the notion that those who shared God's jealousy for God's people should remove from the scene those who were unfaithful to the covenant of God or those who opposed his holy will.

The party of Zealots that was active at the time of Jesus may have had its origin in A.D. 6 or 7, when there was organized resistance to a census ordered by Quirinius. The organization seems to have continued as a protest to the domination of Rome. Zealot militancy was also evident in their desire to help usher in the messianic age. They were devoted to the Law of God and zealous of the interpretation of the Law to the point of death. They were willing to take the lives of fellow Israelites as well as Gentiles rather than transgress the Law.

Some have surmised that Barabbas, who was set free by Pilate at Jesus' trial, was a member of the Zealots, because Luke mentions that he was thrown in prison for insurrection and murder (Luke 23:18-19). The Zealots remained active up to the uprising against Rome in A.D. 66, when they offered fanatical resistance to the Roman army.

Jesus Accepted Simon

There is a hint that Simon the Zealot permitted his influence to be felt among the Twelve. Luke records that when our Lord was giving the disciples last-minute instructions in his farewell discourse, he indicated that they were going into battle with his enemies, who would crucify him along with transgressors. To impress them with the gravity of the situation, he said, "If you don't have a sword, sell your cloak and buy one."

The disciples were quick to respond, "See, Lord, here are two swords."

Jesus said to them, "That is enough" (Luke 22:35-38).

This remarkable exchange between Jesus and the disciples appears to be totally out of character for Jesus. One finds it difficult to imagine that Jesus, who exhorted the disciples to love their enemies and in the garden demonstrated completely different behavior, would have encouraged the use of the sword. His intent may have been to symbolize for the disciples the seriousness of the hour. Some translators have also suggested that when the disciples said they had two swords, Jesus said, "Enough of this!" Whatever Jesus said, he must have smiled at the naivete of the disciples and cried for their lack of understanding.

What is notable, however, is the fact that the Twelve had two swords stashed away. Simon the Zealot may have had one weapon, waiting for the moment when Jesus would signal the beginning of the revolt. Some have suggested that Simon Peter had the other sword, because he used one in the garden (John 18:10), and he, too, may have been a Zealot. But that is speculation. What we know is that Jesus had called Simon the Zealot to be one of his disciples. He made room for the man and his sword and allowed him to see how he would usher in the great messianic day.

No Moderate

The presence of Simon the Zealot in the ranks of the Twelve probably made for some interesting debates. Extremists normally have that effect. Whether on the far right or on the far left, the individual who holds to extreme views sharpens issues and causes people to take sides. For an extremist there appears to be no middle ground, no compromise, no adaptation, no revision. Someone like Simon the Zealot also makes us uncomfortable by forcing issues on us we would like to forget—things we are not sure about, or things on which we hold opposite views.

Simon's Zealotism did not prevail among the disciples. In the Garden of Gethsemane, when Peter drew a sword and cut off an ear of a slave, Jesus quickly put an end to the violence: "Put your sword back in its place," Jesus said to him, "for all who draw the sword will die by the sword. Do you think I cannot call on my Father, and he will at once put at my disposal more than twelve legions of angels? But how then would the Scriptures be fulfilled that say it must happen in this way?" (Matt. 26:52-54). At that moment Simon the Zealot was introduced to a new way of looking at life. He discovered that Jesus was willing to submit to death at the hands of others that he might win the trust and love of the world.

Simon Stayed On

Simon stayed on to witness that our Lord Jesus Christ did reconcile the world to God the Father by his death and resurrection. Simon the Zealot learned that people cannot be intimidated into believing. The true nature of God is not that he is all-powerful, but that he is all-loving.

Simon the Zealot was there to share the glorious news of the resurrection (John 20:19). He was present for the ascension (Acts 1:1-11). He was present when the apostles elected a substitute for Judas Iscariot (Acts 1:23-26). At Pentecost he was empowered to be a witness to the risen Christ as the Lord and Savior of all people (Acts 2).

Our information about Simon the Zealot after Pentecost runs parallel to the traditions about Thaddaeus. Legends place the two in Armenia, where they reportedly worked with some success before their martyrdom.

Simon the Zealot and Us

What is important to us is that Simon the Zealot was called to be a part of the group to whom Jesus entrusted the gospel. Jesus made room for the kind of person who has radical notions about spiritual things. They, too, can be won by his love just as we have to be won and forgiven by his grace for the erroneous ideas we have.

Like Paul after he had seen the risen Christ, Simon the Zealot was consumed with zeal to serve his Lord, but now in *spiritual* warfare. Paul urges us to use the same kind of zeal for the same purpose. "Stand firm then, with the belt of truth buckled around your waist, with the breastplate of righteousness in place, and with your feet fitted with the readiness that comes from the gospel of peace. In addition to all this, take up the shield of faith, with which you can extinguish all the flaming arrows of the evil one. Take the helmet of salvation and the sword of the Spirit, which is the word of God" (Eph. 6:14-17).

When Judas, who had betrayed him, saw that Jesus was condemned, he was seized with remorse and returned the thirty silver coins to the chief priests and the elders. "I have sinned," he said, "for I have betrayed innocent blood."

"What is that to us?" they replied. "That's your responsibility."

Matthew 27:3-4

THIRTEEN

JUDAS ISCARIOT, THE ENIGMA

The surnames of some of the disciples have helped us discover insights into their personalities. In the case of Judas Iscariot, the opposite is true. There is considerable question as to what the designation *Iscariot* means. The most widely held interpretation is that he is the "man from Kerioth." Though the location of Kerioth is not certain, Judas may have been so identified to indicate that he was the only one of the Twelve to hail from Judea. Other explanations of Iscariot are "the assassin," the "carrier of the leather bag," or the "false one." The latter explanation is plausible since the translation may be from the Aramaic word that means "false one, liar, or hypocrite." One can readily understand why the evangelists would hang such an epithet on the one who betrayed their master. However, we must admit that the real meaning of the name Iscariot remains a mystery.

Another Mystery

Almost everything else about Judas Iscariot is also a mystery. Why did Jesus choose Judas as a disciple? How could Jesus, who demonstrated amazing insights into the characters of people, miscalculate so seriously about Judas?

Judas seems to have held an important place in the circle of the Twelve in the beginning. He was elected or chosen treasurer of the movement (John 12:6; 13:29). The account of the Passover in the Upper Room suggests that as late as the night in which he betrayed Jesus, Judas may have been reclining alongside him or at least very close to him (John 13:21-27). We are confronted by the fact that one in whom the Lord invested responsibility and on whom the Twelve relied betrayed that trust. What is more striking is the fact that the one who received the same gracious call as the other eleven proved to be unfaithful and betrayed Jesus.

That this was a disturbing question for the early church is obvious from the several references in the gospel of John (6:70-71; 12:4-6; 13:2-4, 13-27) that suggest that the betrayal by Judas was part of God's plan of salvation.

A Common Complaint

The behavior of Judas Iscariot before the betrayal does not in itself make him suspect. In retrospect, John said that Judas' protest of the anointing of Jesus at Bethany by Mary was purely selfish (John 12:1-6). After the fact, it had become apparent to the Twelve that Judas Iscariot had been a thief as well as a betrayer. But at the time, Judas Iscariot had simply asked, "Why wasn't this perfume sold and the money given to the poor?" (John 12:5).

Many would have agreed with Judas. Today people echo his complaint when they are asked to give for a new church building, for an organ to enhance the congregation's worship, for a painting or sculpture to illustrate the faith, or for other aesthetic gifts by which people demonstrate their devotion and love for the Lord. Judas has furnished many people with an argument to use in fighting for lower budgets in their congregations. We should remember that Jesus responded by saying that Christians can do both: they can always give to the poor and still do something special for their Lord (12:7-8).

The Evil Plot

There is no mystery about the plot that Judas hatched with Jesus' enemies to take him into custody. Judas went to the chief priests and bargained with them, to make Jesus accessible to them for a price. They agreed on the sum of 30 pieces of silver (Matt. 26:14-16), and the arranged signal was a kiss (vv. 48-50). Mark 14:10-11 and Luke 22:3-6 do not mention the amount of the contract, but they note the delight the chief priests took in this breakthrough.

Mark and Luke also mention the prearranged signal. Mark does not mention Jesus' reaction to the kiss (14:44-46), but Luke tells us that Jesus asked the question, "Judas, are you betraying the Son of Man with a kiss?" (22:47-48). Luke 22:30 mentions that it was Satan who prompted Judas to this nefarious deed. John appears to be more interested in that fact rather than stressing the details of the plot (13:2, 27). Yet it is John who gives the impression that Judas was the one who picked the hour, named the rendezvous, led the troops, and stood with them through the arrest (18:2-6).

His Motives

The motive for Judas' betrayal of Jesus remains a mystery. John's observation that Judas Iscariot was a thief suggests that he may have done it out of greed (12:6). It could be, however, that Judas had been completely frustrated by the manner in which Jesus was handling his mission. He may have entertained high hopes of being part of the group who could usher in the messianic age. The year of popularity our Lord had enjoyed was rich in promise for one who was enthusiastic about the kingdom promised by God. Jesus had fired up the imagination of the Twelve with the signs of his mastery over the creation. However, things turned sour during the last year of that ministry. Tension mounted between Jesus and his enemies, and Jesus appeared to denounce the whole system of the religious community. That may have been too much for Judas. Each of the evangelists agree that Judas took the initiative in going to the chief priests. He defected from the Lord's ranks and went over to the other side.

Another theory suggests that Judas was the most devout follower of Jesus. He may have believed that it was important for him to set the stage in which Jesus could demonstrate his messiahship by overthrowing the opposition. In betraying Jesus, Judas could advance the cause of the kingdom in the very way all the Twelve had thought it would come.

The evangelists, however, do not explain the motives of Judas. They simply report the deed and hold him responsible.

His Fate

The fate of Judas is also something of a mystery. Neither Mark nor John say anything about what happened to Judas. Matthew reports that when Judas saw the Lord condemned, he was sorry for what had taken place as a result of treachery. He returned to the chief priests, perhaps with the wild scheme to reverse what he had done. The chief priests refused to listen to him, so Judas threw the money back at them and went out and hanged himself. They took the money and used it to buy a cheap burial ground for foreigners (Matt. 27:3-10).

Luke reports that when Peter informed the disciples of what happened to Judas, he said that Judas had purchased a field with his traitorous reward (Acts 1:15-20). Peter went on to report that Judas had fallen headlong and that his body "burst open and all his intestines gushed out," as a result of which the piece of land which he had bought came to be known as the Field of Blood (Acts 1:16-20).

His Real Sin

As heinous as the crime was that Judas Iscariot committed when he delivered Jesus into the hands of his enemies, it was not the sin that condemned him. Other members of the Twelve forsook Jesus and fled (Matt. 26:56; Mark 14:50). Soldiers mocked him and beat him (Matt. 27:27-31; Mark 14:65; Luke 22:63; John 19:1-3). Peter denied him vociferously (Matt. 26:69-75; Mark 14:66-72; Luke 22:54-62; John 18:15-18, 25-27). Paul confessed that he had been the worst sinner of all and was unfit for the apostolate because he had persecuted the church of God (1 Cor. 15:9). Peter laid the judgment on all people: "You killed the author of life" (Acts 3:15). Yet from the cross the Lord interceded for all who had wronged him: "Father, forgive them, for they do not know what they are doing" (Luke 23:34).

Paul later explained that through the cross, "God was reconciling the world to himself in Christ, not counting men's sins against them" (2 Cor. 5:19). Judas was included in that act of reconciliation no less than others. From the evidence we have, it appears that he did not believe that.

Peter did and was reinstated as an apostle (John 21:15-19). The other disciples did and were also recommissioned by the Lord (Acts 1:8). Judas could have been back in his old place among the Twelve, but his guilt and grief led him to despair. It was unbelief that damned him. The grace, love, and forgiveness of Jesus is greater than the worst of sins. "Where sin increased, grace increased all the more" (Rom. 5:20).

Judas Iscariot and Us

The call of Judas signals to us that God wants everyone to experience the wonders of his grace and love. Furthermore, God does not exclude us because we commit some spiritual blunder. If he did, no one could be called. God works with us in spite of our failures, sins, and shortcomings. God redeems the worst of our miscues and can work them to his advantage. God does not predestine to evil. When our sinful abuse of our will collides with God's mercy, God can win us back with love and forgiveness.

Judas Iscariot also illustrates for us how prone we are to worship our grief and guilt more than God. When we permit our despair to rule us, we do not honor God. Repentance is not simply feeling sorry. It is not confession and the determination to sin no more. True repentance is turning from our sorrow for sin to the one alone who is able to atone for our sin. Therefore, "since we have been justified by faith, we have peace with God through our Lord Jesus Christ" (Rom. 5:1). No one need be cut off from God, no matter how great the sin. We can be saved in spite of ourselves, because he has done what needed to be done. We need only repent and believe.

*In those days Peter stood up among the believers (a
group numbering about a hundred and twenty), and
said, "Brothers, the Scripture had to be fulfilled which
the Holy Spirit spoke long ago through the mouth of
David concerning Judas, who served as guide for those
who arrested Jesus—he was one of our number and
shared in this ministry. . . .*

*"Therefore it is necessary to choose one of the men
who have been with us the whole time Jesus went in and
out among us, beginning from John's baptism to the time
when he was taken up from us. For one of these must
become a witness with us of his resurrection."*

*So they proposed two men: Joseph called Barsabbas,
(also known as Justus) and Matthias. Then they prayed,
"Lord, you know everyone's heart. Show us which of
these two you have chosen to take over this apostolic
ministry, which Judas left to go where he belongs." Then
they drew lots, and the lot fell to Matthias; so he was
added to the eleven apostles.*

Acts 1:15-17, 21-26

FOURTEEN

MATTHIAS, THE REPLACEMENT

The loss of Judas Iscariot from the ranks of the Twelve was keenly felt. The eleven and their families and friends must have felt grief and profound shock at the death of their former associate. A suicide is usually accompanied by some sense of guilt on the part of family and friends, who wonder if they could have done something to prevent the tragedy.

At the same time, the disciples were still in a confused state about the significance of Jesus' resurrection. At Easter, when the risen Christ was present among them, "they still did not believe for joy and amazement" (Luke 24:41). They were elated for the victory that had been gained by the Lord, but they were not sure of themselves and were under instructions from Jesus to remain in the city until they were "clothed with power from on high" (Luke 24:49).

In addition, the disciples felt the burden of replacing Judas Iscariot, because of the importance attached to the number 12. Jesus had made it clear to the disciples that just as there had been 12 tribes of Israel through whom God would bless all the nations of the earth, 12 apostles were to be instruments through whom God would proclaim the good news to all the earth. Jesus had entrusted to the Twelve this great mission (John 14:25-27; Matt. 10:1-42). He had promised the Twelve that in his kingdom they would sit on 12 thrones, judging the 12 tribes of Israel (Matt. 19:28; Luke 22:30). It is no wonder that the first item on the agenda for the Twelve after the Lord's ascension was to find a replacement for Judas Iscariot and keep the movement intact.

The Criteria

The decision to look for a replacement prompted Peter to set down criteria that would shape the selection. The job description and qualifications were drawn up with prudence and sagacity: "It is necessary to choose one of the men who have been with us the whole time Jesus went in and out among us, beginning from John's baptism to the time when he was taken up from us. For one of these must become a witness with us of his resurrection" (Acts 1:21-22). Peter said that this replacement had been indicated in the Psalms (Acts 1:20). From the manner in which Peter quotes from Psalms 69:25 and 109:8, one can picture how the disciples read and reread the Hebrew scriptures anew in the light of all that had been revealed in the Lord Jesus.

It was clear to them that they needed someone who could bear witness to all they had heard and seen in the life, death, and resurrection of Jesus. His mission and ministry had to continue. The person to be chosen would have to be one of their associates who could also be acknowledged as a peer by what he had witnessed.

The Candidates

After Peter had announced the plan for a replacement for Judas Iscariot and had enunciated the qualifications, two candidates were proposed: Joseph called Barsabbas (also known as Justus) and Matthias (Acts 1:23). These two probably emerged from the ranks of the seventy (or seventy-two) whom the Lord had appointed as a vanguard in his mission efforts (Luke 10:1). They had been sent out in pairs and had been instructed by Jesus in a seminar on evangelism. Their campaign had been a success, and they returned with joy to report to our Lord with considerable enthusiasm (Luke 10:17).

Matthew mentions that in their first mission the Twelve had been paired off in the same manner as the seventy (Matt. 10:1-40). The Twelve may have felt the urgency to round out their numbers to twelve once more because they planned to go out in teams of two again. We can also surmise that the candidates who were put forth would have been from the seventy, because they would have had previous experience in the earlier evangelism effort. Certainly Joseph and Matthias were also a part of that circle of about 120 who appeared to gather regularly in the Upper Room after the resurrection (Acts 1:20). What made their credentials impeccable, however, was the fact that they had been identified with the Lord's mission from the beginning and were good candidates to be teamed up with any one of the apostles as witnesses to what they had seen and heard.

The Election

After Peter led the group in prayer they drew lots to decide which of the two would fill the vacancy (Acts 1:26).

The two names were probably placed on stones, which were deposited in a bottle. The bottle was shaken, and the first to fall out was the chosen one. It could be that they "gave" lots. In that event, they would have been voting.

If the group followed the first procedure, which was the more likely, some might think of that as being rather primitive and unsophisticated. However, the procedure was not as chancy as one might think. The limited ballot would indicate that much thought had already been given to the selection of the two candidates. Furthermore, a proper prayer was spoken. Missionaries who have observed these methods in primitive communities have reported that the benefit of this method is that often the more faithful and more capable candidate has won out over the popular candidate.

The Answer to Prayer

The outcome of the election by lots was that Matthias was added to the eleven apostles. The willingness and readiness to accept this result was in large measure due to the prayer led by Peter. He had prayed, "Lord, you know everyone's heart. Show us which one of these two you have chosen to take over this apostolic ministry which Judas left" (Acts 1:24-25). The prayer is noteworthy, because it is the first recorded corporate prayer spoken by the disciples after the resurrection. The prayer indicates to us that the disciples took seriously both the command and the promise Jesus had spoken to them as he prepared them for the time when he would return to the Father (John 16:23-24). The resurrection of Jesus had emboldened the disciples and given them resources that were completely new to them.

The prayer is also significant for its pattern. This is no long recital that relies on its own uniqueness or beauty to influence God. Like the ancient and brief collects of the church, the prayer states its confidence that God already knows the situation and has the power to do something about it, and then makes the request with an explicit petition. That, too, reflected the heart of the discourse the Lord gave on prayer (Matt. 6:5-15), and stands as a model for economy of words in our prayers.

In the end, all could say that Matthias was an answer to prayer. This young and vibrant community of believers could feel confident that Matthias was the one whom God had hand-picked for the apostolate.

The Apostolate Continues

Not everyone agrees that Matthias was God's choice. Some have suggested that the Jerusalem Christians made a serious mistake in selecting someone to take Judas Iscariot's place. They reason that the community of the Upper Room had been too anxious, and that they failed to believe that God himself would choose a replacement for Judas Iscariot. They point out that God did that when he called Saul and elected him to be the apostle Paul (Acts 9:1-19). That theory, of course, rests on a literalistic and limited view of the apostolate not shared by the New Testament.

The disciples felt the importance of organizing themselves for the commission which Christ had given them (Matt. 28:19-20; Luke 24:48-49; John 20:21-23; Acts 1:8) and doing so in the manner in which they had been trained (Matt. 10:1-42; Luke 10:1-16). They needed to be twelve. However, later the idea of the apostolate was stretched beyond the band of twelve. Paul insisted on his credentials as an apostle who performed all the signs of the apostle and also spoke of false apostles (2 Cor. 11:13). He also referred to James, the brother of the Lord, and to Barnabas, Paul's coworker, as apostles (1 Cor. 9:5-6). For Paul, the apostles were those who were witnesses to the risen Christ and had a special calling to serve the purpose of God for the salvation of all.

Empowered by the Spirit

The selection of Matthias to fill the vacancy left by Judas Iscariot happened just in time. No sooner had Matthias been initiated as the twelfth apostle, when the Twelve experienced the miracle of Pentecost. Matthias was present for the outpouring of the Holy Spirit (Acts 2:1,14), and participated in the marvels of that day.

There is nothing to suggest that Matthias lost his place among the Twelve when Paul and James took leading roles in the Christian effort. Rather, the last that the Scriptures have to say about Matthias is that as the replacement for Judas Iscariot, he closed the number which was not to be added to again.

One legend records that Matthias was an active preacher in Judea, and that he was stoned to death by the people there. Another tradition reports that he was one of the five apostles who carried the gospel to Armenia.

Passing on the Faith

The beauty of the story of Matthias is that someone was called up from the ranks to fill this important role in the Lord's missionary effort. Matthias had been present for the public ministry of Jesus which culminated in his death and resurrection. He must have thanked God over and over again for the privilege of being a part of that great ministry. He was called on not because of what he had done. His credentials were that he had been a witness to what God had done in and through the life of Jesus of Nazareth. He was shaped for the apostolate by what Christ did.

Sometimes we feel like hangers-on. We feel like we are not a part of things or that we are just on the periphery. We need to take the focus off ourselves in order to become what we can be. We must recognize that we can be helpful and meaningful in the world because we know Jesus Christ. That puts us up front where we can witness to the saving acts of God.

The story of Matthias is a sign that the apostolate continued with the reestablishment of the Twelve. The next generation, however, was not twelve, but many more. So it should continue on to the end of time as the apostolic faith is preserved among us and shared with others to be passed on from faith to faith, from one generation to the next.

EPILOG

The hints and clues about the Twelve we can uncover in the four Gospels are interesting but not always conclusive. The restraint with which the evangelists treat the personalities of the Twelve is noteworthy. They are not drawn in heroic proportions. Instead, they are ordinary people with feet of clay, whose lives highlight the richness and fullness of Christ's grace and love.

The focus of the evangelists is on the gospel itself. In Jesus of Nazareth God was reconciling the world to himself. The Twelve knew they were living in the presence of that revelation. Though they did not fully understand that Jesus' messiahship would climax in his death and resurrection, they were faithful to him through the good years and the bad.

For the Twelve, Pentecost was the dawning of the realization of what they had experienced in the company of their Master. That was the time for them to launch a missionary enterprise that soon encompassed the world they knew.

The missionary activities of the Twelve are remembered in legends and spurious documents that pose as gospels, books of acts, apocalypses, and traditions. These apocryphal works were attempts by Christians of the second, third, and later centuries to claim apostolic authority and validity for the arrival of the gospel in their lands. These exaggerated stories and legendary tales, intended to heighten the importance of the roles of the Twelve, were unnecessary.

The fate of the apostles was described by our Lord in his farewell discourse to them (John 15:18-27). They were assured God's continued benediction and providence in Jesus' high priestly prayer (John 17:6-19). By that prayer the Lord not only consecrated the Twelve to God but he prayed that we also might be included with them:

My prayer is not for them alone. I pray also for those who will believe in me through their message, that all of them may be one, Father, just as you are in me, and I am in you. May they also be in us, so that the world may believe that you have sent me.

John 17:20-21